The King of Growth

Praise for 8 Figure Firm
and Luis Raul Scott, Jr.

Luis has single handedly helped me scale my business by 10x. The knowledge, the confidence in my abilities to run a 7-figure business and continue scaling up would not have been possible without Luis and the mentorship he has provided. I've had business coaches in the past, but none has had such an impact in my personal and business life. I highly recommend using 8 Figure Firm if you are looking to scale your business and have a good time while you do it.

Armando Leduc
Leduc Entertainment

Luis has been a driving force behind my firm's success. Luis helps me solve problems I didn't know existed and he consistently causes me to uplevel my leadership skill set and my decision making process. The team exhibits the highest level of customer service I have ever experienced. Information is always accurate, responses to issues turn around very fast and are always delivered with respect and concern for my business' future.

Charlotte Christian
Charlotte Christian Law

Luis has been instrumental in setting the foundation for our law practice to scale and achieve unprecedented growth. *In less than one (1) year ... we were able to increase our retainers by over 50% and increase our top-line revenue by over 23%.* This year, we're on pace to double those numbers. Gone are the days of being understaffed, overworked, with only incremental growth to show for it. Now we have a law business that works for us."

David Benn
Work Injury Rights

The phrase of "implementation" that 8FF focuses on has been vital to our growth. They do a great job of simplifying issues to small steps that are doable in implementing. *Luis has been a great help in helping us double last year and having a run rate to double again this year.*

Jorge Virguez
Barrios and Virquez

After working with Luis for one year, I have grown 138%. The focus on staying in marketing and sales until I had someone that could replicate my sales ability allowed me to prevent losing leads and really growing the revenue. Ultimately this led to having better people on the team.

Felicia Bunbury
FAB Law Firm

When I hired Luis, I was experiencing so much employee turnover. In addition to this, I was getting burned out from having to do all of the marketing, consults, sales and legal work. After just one year of working with Luis, I was able to hire an incredible team, reduce turnover and hire several lawyers. *We have now gone from $65,000 in revenue per month to $167,000 in revenue per month in just one year!*

Ayesha Chidolue
The Chidolue Law Firm

Luis Scott's coaching helped me grow my law firm from $785,000 in sales to $4.1M in 24 months! My law firm helps companies and individuals start and grow nonprofits that impact the world. The fact that he could help my firm grow even though we're in a very unique market proves that he can help any business grow. He is the real deal!"

Audrey K. Chisholm
Chisholm Law Firm, PLLC

THE KING

OF

GROWTH

How to Dominate Your Market, Increase
Predictability, and Unleash the Power of Your
Law Firm for Personal and Financial Freedom

LUIS RAUL SCOTT, JR.

The Foundry Press
Columbus, Georgia

ISBN - 978-1-94-222140-1 (pb)

An imprint of Scott Publishing Services
Columbus, Georgia

scottpublishingservices@gmail.com

Dedication

To Rachel, Ruly, Lincoln and Emory.

TABLE OF CONTENTS

ACKNOWLEDGMENTS

This book could not have been possible without the amazing team I have at Bader Scott Injury Lawyers and 8 Figure Firm Consulting.

My wife, Rachel, for your loving support during those moments where I was feeling totally inadequate to even write the book.

Seth Bader for being such an amazing business partner and giving me the freedom and flexibility to shine in my passion for teaching.

Adam Kosloff for having your team at Virtuoso work around the clock to edit this book.

My brother, Victor, Scott Publishing Services, and The Foundry Press for putting this book out into the world.

To my parents who have always encouraged me to believe that I was made for something great.

To my clients who have brought the principles of this book to life in practice.

Thank you! Thank you! Thank you!

INTRODUCTION

"It's not in the dreaming, it's in the doing."

Mark Cuban

There are 1.3 million lawyers in the United States. Many of them want to have a thriving law business but don't know how. The space has become more competitive than ever. In the last two years alone, I have seen dozens upon dozens of lawyers going out on their own to try their hand at this game of law. With new ways to market, especially on social media, it has become much easier for people with no budget to market themselves successfully. Add in a little bit of entertainment and networking and you can have a recipe for a fast-growing law firm in no time. Despite the ease of entry, the difficulty of growing and sustaining a law business has not changed. With this increased competition, becoming profitable and staying profitable has become more challenging today than ever before. Over the last 20 years I have learned what it takes to build a predictable and profitable law firm that can have you working less, making more, and living the life you always dreamed of.

Introduction

To be honest, I never thought it was possible to build a business as big as our law firm. For many years I believed that just having a $2 to $3 million business was all that was attainable. I lived in a small town, I graduated from a small school, and I worked at a relatively small law firm.

When I started out as an attorney, I had big dreams. I dreamed I would work hard and then, as I grew in my role at my firm, I'd be able to step back and take more time for fun and family while continuing to see the rewards of the sweat equity I'd invested in my career. Unfortunately, this outcome did not happen organically. And because I had never scripted my law firm growth, and had never developed a law firm to grow with intentionality, my law firm was not prepared to provide me with the lifestyle that I wanted.

Several years ago though, I had a wake-up call. I realized I needed to grow my firm's business exponentially; otherwise, I would never reap the benefits of the lifestyle I'd dreamed of. Instead, I would continue to burn the candle at both ends until I retired. The beginning of this journey is what led me to write *The 8 Figure Law Firm: The 9 Principles to Exponential Growth.*

For context, I'd been with my former law firm since finishing my undergraduate degree in my early 20s. I started as a receptionist and part-time Spanish interpreter. I honestly wasn't sure if I was even smart enough to be a lawyer. But I knew I wanted to own a business one day. For years my parents told me they thought I would be a lawyer. So, one day, driving down the road, I made the decision to take the LSAT. Two weeks later I was sitting in a room taking the test. I did not know what to expect. But I did well enough to get accepted into several schools, and I decided to go to school part-time at night.

I knew what hard work was all about. I went to work during the day and law school at night four days per week. I studied on the weekends. If that wasn't already enough on my plate, I added the additional stress of having my first baby during my second year of law school. Nevertheless, I made it out and was ready to tackle the rigorous life of being a lawyer.

I expected that my first years practicing law would be busy, and I was right. What I didn't realize was that it wouldn't become much easier as I advanced. Well into my career, I found I was still working long hours in an "eat what you kill" industry where the firm's generated income didn't create a comfortable cushion, at least not the kind I'd dreamed about while I toiled my way through my first few years of practice. I began to wonder how I could improve my firm's business.

After the first several years of being a lawyer, I did not really see any progress in our business. Again, we were in a small town, and for all practical purposes, we were very successful. We had a great reputation and a steady stream of referral business. But something wasn't clicking. We were not really growing. Every year we had the same number of clients and the same revenue. The dream of awesome vacations and second homes was disappearing right before my eyes—not because I was not making a comfortable living but because I WAS making a comfortable living. That was the problem. Everything about my life had become too comfortable. To grow a big business, you have to be willing to make yourself incredibly uncomfortable. I started out trying to analyze what I was doing right and what I was doing wrong.

At first, I wasn't sure what we were doing wrong. We did nearly $3 million in business annually, and we had a few dozen employees. We got great results for our clients, and we stayed busy in a midsized market—but something was off. While I grew in my role with my firm, the firm didn't grow with me. It stayed the same size, and the workload remained heavy. Of course, you expect to be busy when you're a lawyer, but the old adage to "work smarter, not harder" was always in the back of my mind, and I struggled to figure out how the firm could become a business instead of just a job.

Introduction

I realized that the firm I worked for needed to grow—a lot. I dove into seminars, webinars, books, and even hired consultants. In my 15 years with the law firm, I read almost 300 books on business and self-development. Then, I decided to join a consultant group, a group that could teach me how to grow my business in a major way. After joining this group, I realized I needed to be more intentional about everything in the law firm.

I spent more than two years pouring time, energy, and money into trying to grow our firm, yet I kept spinning my wheels. I doubled down and focused solely on business strategy as the firm's managing partner. I was exhausted and disheartened. I had become frustrated at what I believed was an alignment problem. The leadership of the business was not aligned in how to grow the organization. I wanted a business plan and budget and leadership team and meetings. But not everyone was on the same page.

One day, everything came to a head when the firm's other partners asked that I leave the partnership. It was a powerful blow. I didn't complain or cry or defend myself. I knew the partnership had been over for a long time. For more than four years, friends, family, and consultants had been telling me it was only a matter of time before this would happen. So even though I hoped I was going to retire from the only law firm I had ever worked for, I knew that this moment was coming. After the brief meeting, I got up and went home. (That's where the crying happened.)

In all seriousness, I was truly devasted. I felt like I was losing everything I had worked so hard for. I felt my entire identity was wrapped up in this law firm. Everyone in the community knew me as the lawyer who worked at this one office. I had grown up there. Despite the breakup, I have nothing but incredible love and admiration for the colleagues I spent 15 years with there. This firm was where I learned everything about life, law, and business.

But that doesn't mean it wasn't incredibly difficult. I now needed to figure out how I was going to make money.

I know that so far, my story doesn't sound like a success story. But what I've told you up to this point is what inspired me to write this book. I know there are law firm owners out there struggling like I was, wondering how they will be able to take their business to the next level and asking themselves how it is possible to get off the rat race of life. If you feel like you're at a loss and don't know if there's a better way forward in growing your firm, I'm here to tell you that there is and I want to show you how to do it.

The Story Continues

Now, this is where my story gets good—where I was able to start *doing* instead of just *dreaming*. After leaving the firm where I had spent 15 years learning and growing, I started my own firm. And it grew fast.

Within the first 30 days I had 25 clients. Five months later I had over 100 clients and hit $50,000 in revenue. I was taking everything that walked in the door. Child custody, immigration, criminal, probation revocations, workers compensation, personal injury, you name it, I took it. I needed cash in the door as fast as possible. I went to Rotary Club events, was networking like crazy, met several doctors, and dipped into the well of my old referral clients.

It turned out that the knowledge I had gained over the previous 15 years was a secret weapon. The cases I generated brought in over $500,000 in revenue in just five months. But the equity I developed in that time is what took this story into another dimension.

Introduction

Around month five of having my own firm and after two years of talking about this possibility, I teamed up with my best friend to start Bader Scott Injury Lawyers. Four years later, we are on track to doing $32 million in revenue with a pipeline of predictable business valued at almost $40 million.

In this book, I want to share with you the specifics and the mechanics of how we did this.

Did our achievement happen overnight? No. It was, and continues to be, the result of practicing specific techniques in both operations and marketing mindsets that helped us launch successful campaigns and led to a successful business. Our success isn't a fluke—it's grounded in the roadmap I've laid out in this book. The principles in this book have helped dozens of other law firms achieve incredible business success, and they can help you, too.

Don't Be Discouraged

This book is for those who've struggled to grow their firms only to find that their strategies have yielded stagnant or minimal growth. This book is also for the entrepreneurial lawyer who is ready to take their business to the next level and needs a new set of proven ideas that can quickly catapult them forward.

The speed of growth is tied to the speed of implementation.

Don't get me wrong, this isn't a get-rich-quick scheme, and I still work hard. The difference is that now our firm operates as a successful business. To me, a business should be an entity that runs without the owner having to be involved. My involvement is directly tied to my *desire* to be involved—not the *need* to be involved. I go on family vacations, I go to my kids' soccer games, and I can take off whenever I want even as the business continues to grow. The time I spend with my family is no longer burdened with the anxieties that come with unpredictable revenue streams. Our staff and clients are happy, and our firm runs like a well-oiled machine. Sure, the machine requires modification from time to time—but we could set it on cruise control if we wanted without worrying it might break down on the side of the road.

When we decided to take our firm to the next level, we analyzed every facet of running it as a business. From marketing to management, we deconstructed and reconstructed each piece of the puzzle until we found the key components to leverage for optimal growth. We had some great mentors along the way. We learned that vision, mission, and values drive the organization in ways we could have never imagined. Most importantly, we put things into practice. The speed of growth is tied to the speed of implementation. If you want to grow quickly, you need to implement quickly.

In the following chapters, I will break down the strategies that led to our exponential growth. Our success hinged on an astute understanding of the following:

- Law firm growth economics

- The marketing mindset

- Clarifying the customer journey

- Methods for marketing through referrals, social media, and mass media

- Launching and measuring successful marketing campaigns

Who Is This Book For?

This book is for the law firm owner who's tired of spinning their wheels trying to take the growth of their firm to the next level. This book is also for the future law firm owner who wants to get out ahead of their competitors' game before their own initial launch. Whoever you are, you know there's more to running a successful law firm than marginal growth and generating only $2 to $3 million year after year after year. You've seen other firms in similar markets explode in size and revenue, and you want to know if you can do it too. You can.

This book provides practical solutions that are accessible to anyone willing to apply them. While I can't guarantee your success will look exactly like ours, I can promise that you'll experience large growth with less work if you put these principles into practice. You don't need a Ph.D.-level understanding of specialized industry data or an advanced degree in the bells and whistles of the latest algorithms. What you need is a desire to grow your law firm exponentially and the enthusiasm to embrace the principles discussed in this book. Add some intention plus implementation, and you will be scaling in no time.

CHAPTER 1

THE ECONOMICS OF
A LAW BUSINESS

"There is a limit to how much you can cut, but there is no limit to how much you can earn."

Ramit Sethi

When I first started consulting, I really no idea if what I was teaching was going to work for other people. I knew it had worked for me. I had taken my own law firm to a seven-figure run rate in less than five months, and when I joined with my business partner, we went to multiple eight figures in less than three years. But there was something inside of me that still doubted that this could be duplicated by anyone else. And it wasn't pride that carried that doubt. It was a tremendous sense of insecurity that maybe I just was lucky.

However, I really have a passion for consulting and speaking. I wanted to be able to help people experience the exponential growth I saw in my own life with my own law firm. One day I sat down and started to outline what I believed were the key lessons that led to the growth I had experienced in my own life. When I finished, I was 60 pages into a book that I ultimately titled *The 8 Figure Firm: The 9 Principles to Achieve Exponential Growth*. This book became my first lead magnet that I used to try to get new clients. I use the term "magnet" very loosely because I couldn't actually get anyone to read the book, even though I was promoting it to everyone I knew at the time.

Fortunately for me, I had a decent reputation for growing law firms. Because I had spent a tremendous amount of time studying how to grow a law firm, I decided to do a webinar called "5 Things You Should Not Do During the Coronavirus Pandemic." It's crazy to think how long ago that feels.

At this webinar I had 10 attendees, six of whom I believe were employees. It was the first and last time I did a webinar because it felt like such a failure. However, there was one attendee who was a friend of mine. After the webinar she texted me and told me I did a great job. I put everyone on an email follow-up for about four weeks and that was about it. Nothing really came out of it. No one called me or tried to hire me for consulting services. I had spent so much time writing this webinar and developing and recording its five points that I became consumed with the outcome alone and not the value-add. I had always taught that the value-add was the most important part of any business, but I had lost sight of that because I was too invested in the outcome of getting a client to actually hire me. You will learn in this book that one of the biggest mistakes you can make in your marketing is basing all of your marketing on the outcome.

Three months later, this friend sent me another message asking me if I was interested in coaching her in growing her firm. My heart sank immediately. There was no way this person was going to pay me for consulting. I mean, me? I had never consulted anyone before. I was nervous as hell. But I said yes. Then came the true test. She asked me how much I would charge. I remember my business partner telling me at the time that I had a gift. (My love language is words of affirmation, so I think he was just trying to build me up.) I told him about the request, and he asked me what I was going to do. I said, "I'm going to charge $2,000 per month! There was no way she was going to pay this." But she did. She didn't bat an eye. I knew immediately that I had some big shoes to fill, and they were the shoes of the man she expected me to be. After all, she came to me for help and that meant that my success or failure depended on my ability to actually provide the help.

Immediately, we started working together. One of the first things I shared was the economics of marketing and the importance of marketing your firm using the formula I am about to provide you in this book. After implementing many of the strategies that I outline in this book, my very first client grew her business from $700,000 in revenues per year to $2.4 million in revenues in the first year working with me. She is now on track to become one of my first firms to reach eight figures in predictable revenues. It was then that I knew that the formula worked. Not just for me but for everyone. Her firm wasn't even a personal injury firm. I then knew that it could work for anyone who used the formula correctly.

Since then, I have taught this formula to dozens of law firms in various practice areas, all of whom have had similar success. Now, no one can guarantee this type of success, but I do know that the people who took this information and implemented it with courage have achieved incredible results because of it. Many of them have claimed that the secrets I taught them have changed their life.

To take your firm to the next level, you must understand the methods of making your law firm grow. And despite what many people may believe, there is a method. The method starts by understanding one core principle of the human condition: "People are predictable." This may be the first time you're hearing this, but people are, in fact, predictable. And not just some people. All people. There is a level of predictability in all of us. Most of us brush our teeth in the morning. This allows toothpaste companies to determine with a degree of specificity how much toothpaste will be sold in a city based on the population. I don't know if they do this, but maybe they should.

Many of us travel in the summers specifically. This is what informs airlines and hotels to beef up staff. When you go to a restaurant they rarely run out of food because they generally know how many people are going to show up on any given night. Recently, I went to a sporting event and the all-you-can eat buffet never seemed to run out of food. Without predictability, there would be no way for these venues to determine the amount of food to cook.

When my wife was planning my 40th birthday party, we asked the venue how much food they would cook for the crowd we had invited and they responded, "2½ pieces per guest." It's all predictable.

People underestimate the compounding effect of consistency over time.

This knowledge gives us the understanding that if you use the formula for your benefit and combine it with the predictability of people, you can create a marketing plan that will work for you. Because people are predictable, almost everything in your business can be predicted with a certain degree of accuracy.

You are also able to predict how many people you will need to hire, how many supplies you will need to purchase, and even how much space you will need for your office.

This predictability is what creates the confidence I have that if you use the economics of law firm growth consistently, you will achieve a predictable outcome over a period of time. The question is not whether it will work for you or your practice area, or even your geographic location. The question is whether or not you have the stamina and belief to implement the system long enough for it to take hold.

One of the hardest things to do as a consultant is prove to a client that the strategy works when it isn't working for them at the same speed that it worked for other people. Unfortunately, just like being a trainer in the gym, it is not enough for me to give you a meal plan and a workout plan for you to develop six-pack abs in three months. For some people it may take three years. And for others it may take 10 years. That does not change the fact that the plan will work if you do it long enough.

To me, the biggest difference between those that grow fast and those that grow slowly is the ability to manage change and implement it quickly. Ultimately, whether you grow quickly or slowly does not change the formula, which has been proven to work for dozens upon dozens of law firms across the country. It's no different than a trainer.

People underestimate the compounding effect of consistency over time. Playing the piano 15 minutes per day for one year may not make you very good at playing the piano. However, playing the same song 15 minutes per day for one year will make you sound like Beethoven for only that one song. The difference is the consistency over time for a very specific activity.

But all too often we give up too quickly because we get weary. We become disenchanted by the results or the lack of results. We do not realize that we are trying to master the piano instead of just mastering the song. And the difference between those two strategies can make all the difference in the success of your law firm. When you begin to focus on just the songs that you need to play to make your law firm successful, you will compound the effect that you need to create momentum in your business. And fast growth requires a tremendous amount of momentum. This seems like common sense, but you would be surprised how many times I have to tell a lawyer to stop focusing on policies and procedures and start focusing on acquiring clients. Developing systems, policies, and procedures has become the scapegoat for law firm owners who fear marketing their law firms or investing in their law firms.

Nevertheless, if you do not master the song, you will become tired of this grind. Before anyone gets to the tired state or stays there, I want to tell you that people are absolutely predictable. You must use the predictability of people to stay focused on your company goals and marketing plans so that the compounding effect that consistency brings will take hold in your business. In addition to staying consistent, the predictability of people will allow you to focus on figuring out the message that your brand needs to communicate to reach your ideal client. Contrary to what many people believe about law firm competition, your ideal client is not the same as your competitor's ideal client, if you share similar characteristics. We will cover this more in the chapter on branding, but part of branding is figuring out your brand appeal. For now, your goal is to use the economics of law firm building to craft a marketing plan that will generate predictable leads.

I understand that economics is a dry topic, but developing an understanding of the basic math of your law firm is the best way to facilitate huge, reliable growth. While you can save money by tightening your budget, you can't exponentially increase profit only by restricting expenditures. If you want exponential growth, you'll need to understand your firm's actual and potential profitability. You must understand how to generate momentum in your business. And yes, we can cut expenditures, and we can create operational efficiencies through leveraging people, but ultimately generating the cases you want requires you to hone in on the formula that I will share here shortly.

Maybe you're already someone who loves deep diving into your law firm's economic equation, or perhaps you're not yet that person. If you're of the latter group, consider viewing law firm economics through a different lens to find motivation. Sure, there are numbers and equations involved, but these analytics are the means to your ultimate end: an 8 Figure Firm. Do not overlook this chapter. It explains how to use the predictability of human nature to craft a virtually guaranteed successful marketing plan.

Why do we want to understand the economics of law firm growth from the outset of the journey? The answer is that certain metrics—like margins, contributions, case acquisition costs, and marketing budgets all contribute to overall profitability. The formula matters. Understanding the formula and having the confidence to execute it will determine the speed at which your firm rises.

Just to be clear, everything I am teaching is not only what we did to build our law firm but also the steps we took to build 8 Figure Firm Consulting, which became a multi-seven figure business in 20 months. In addition to this, we've helped dozens upon dozens of law firms double and triple their revenue. Many of them doubled and tripled seven figures of revenue year over year. I say all of this not to boast but rather to give you confidence: many people have taken the leap and have found tremendous success by implementing what I'm about to share with you in this next section.

It's Just Math!

There was a time when I did not understand the game of law firm building. I couldn't figure out how to actually develop a predictable book of business. I spent a lot of years studying how other businesses develop their leads. What I found out during that time is that every product required a specific amount of investment in order to be successfully brought to the market. What many law firm owners fail to realize is that a practice area of law is simply a product. If you are a family lawyer, your product is family law. If you are a personal injury lawyer, your product is personal injury law. And if you practice multiple disciplines in your business, you have multiple products.

In every situation, deciding how much should be allocated to your marketing budget isn't a guessing game; it's a math problem. This is good news! For far too long, law firms have depended on the referral strategy for building their business. They thought if they had a good product, people would come. And to some extent having a good product is part of this. But that is only a fraction of running and scaling a successful law firm. The most important part of scaling your firm is understanding how you create predictability and momentum. That does not come from simply relying on the referrals.

What Should You Spend on Marketing?

Based on the predictability of people, if your plan is to create momentum and your desire is to scale your business, I recommend you spend 25 percent of last year's revenue on marketing for the upcoming year, with an upward trajectory throughout the year that increases as your revenues increase. I will explain how to prepare your marketing budget in a later chapter. The first thing you have to calculate before you start on your marketing journey is the amount of money you are going to spend in the new year. If your revenue the previous year was $500,000, then your marketing budget in the new year would be no less than 25 percent of that number, or $125,000.

If your revenue in the previous year was $1 million, then 25 percent of that would be no less than $250,000. As your revenue increases over the year, you would reevaluate on a quarterly basis and increase for the new quarter based on the moving run rate. This formula will create momentum. In later chapters we will discuss how to use the formula and how to create a plan to achieve the maximum outcome.

If you believe this sounds aggressive, I want you to remember the objective: to scale and grow your law firm quickly. One of the biggest challenges in the law firm industry is that law firm owners get too comfortable taking home 50 percent of the revenues being generated. This type of profit margin will never lead to a fast-growing organization because the money that could and should be reinvested in the company is being taken for the benefit of the owners.

This is the number that builds momentum while also considering your growth from the prior year. I know in working with many clients that this can seem like a crazy and scary proposition, especially if you are accustomed to getting most of your business without much effort. However, one of the most important parts of scaling your firm to eight figures is having the courage to make uncomfortable decisions.

There are other ratios you should keep in mind as well. Specifically, I teach law firm owners to keep payroll at around 37 to 40 percent and operations around 10 to 12 percent. If you add up the numbers, spending on the high end, owners are taking 23 percent home; spending on the low end, owners are keeping 28 percent. Again, this doesn't sound like a lot of profit compared to taking home 50 percent—which is where many slow-growing law firms live and eventually die—but the only way to create momentum, predictability, and a law business that pays you for life is to turn it into a client-generation machine.

One of the reasons I started 8 Figure Firm Consulting is because I knew if you could make it to $10 million in **PREDICTABLE** revenues, you would have a business that was better than any investment you could ever imagine. I saw that as the point of no return, the pivotal point where you would never have to go back to working cases, where the business ran without you, and where the cases flowed consistently year after year.

How Can I Afford This?

Several years ago, I was working with a client who could not get out of the way and spend more than 10 percent on marketing. They believed that they had too much business already. You might be thinking that's a nice problem to have. I continued to stress the importance of creating momentum and predictability in the marketing and using it not only to create more revenue and profit as well as consistency in lead generation.

One day it happened. The very thing I told him would happen came true. His leads and signups were going down and he was losing all of the momentum he had in new client acquisition. It was a terrible to sit there and see it all unfold.

We didn't cry a river about it. We just got up and worked the marketing plan and made the commitment to start spending the money that was necessary to make the business grow.

You might be worried that spending a quarter of your revenue on marketing will reduce your profit by 25 percent, but remember, marketing produces a return on investment. The key is knowing the cost of acquisition for your product and the expected return for that sale.

Let's assume some numbers to illustrate how this would work. For the purposes of this illustration, let's assume that your cost of acquisition is $1,000 per case and your average case fee is $5,000. In this assumption, you decide to take your marketing from 10 percent of revenues to 25 percent of revenues as I generally recommend. The increase in marketing spend would see you spending an additional $25,000 per month. In this analysis, we know that the revenues for this firm are $166,000 ($25,000 divided by the additional 15 percent we are spending).

Doing the math, what we see is that a rise in $25,000 marketing spend would result in 25 new cases acquired. ($25,000/$1,000 per case). Those same cases would produce $125,000 in additional new revenue (25 cases at $5,000 per case). Assuming the earning time was one month, we would increase the revenues in the first month by $125,000. Assuming the earning time was three months, we would increase the earnings by $125,000 in the first quarter with the increased spend. And lastly, assuming the earning period was one year, the $125,000 would be earned over 12 months.

If this is possible, and it is, how much money would you invest into your marketing? The answer is probably, "As much as I could get my hands on!"

This is one of the reasons my business partner and I have been so bullish on our business the last few years. Once we learned the right brand appeal, message, marketing campaign mix, and resulting cost of acquisition, all that was left was to make the investment to see the return.

Once you have done this several times in a year, and preferably for the entire year and not just one month, in the following year you will be able to incorporate the new revenue into your marketing budget and reap even more benefits from the investment. This positive feedback loop is how exponential growth happens. This is how you become an 8 Figure Firm.

The Challenge

You may be thinking, "If this is so easy, why doesn't everyone just do it?"

First, it is because most law firm owners do not know their cost of acquisition. Without knowing the true cost of acquisition, it is impossible to know how many cases your investment will yield. If you do not know how many cases your investment will yield, it is impossible to determine what type of revenue you will generate. Revenue generation is a vital part of not only profitability but also the ability to sustain the business as you create more and more efficiencies.

Figuring out the cost of acquisition is no small task. If you have spent the majority of your time marketing by referral, you will have difficulty knowing the cost of acquisition in the open market when you are competing against other law firms that do the same thing that you do. Herein lies the second problem.

Second, most law firm owners do not want to take the time to figure out their cost of acquisition. They view spending money to test the market as a waste of money. To some extent they may be right because you are essentially wasting money to see if your message, brand, or product is worth anything in the open market.

When I first started 8 Figure Firm, we had a group coaching model which I thought would be a big hit. We were spending $12,000 per month marketing the coaching, but I was having difficulty convincing people to sign up for the program. What we learned is that the sales pitch was all wrong and we needed to do something else. After making the changes and refining our message, we had a big hit. If you are not willing to invest to find your brand's cost of acquisition, you may be sitting on the sidelines for a very long time while your competition discovers theirs and uses it to their advantage.

The third reason is that many law firms have not spent enough time identifying their brand, message, or strategy and therefore this level of predictability does not exist in their current business. In order to have predictability in lead generation, you must know your brand appeal, message, and strategy, and know what cost of acquisition those three lead to. If you are doubting this is possible, I can tell you with certainty that it is because people are predictable. It is not how good your message is, although this helps. It is not how good your product is, although this helps. It is not how good your brand is, although this also helps. It is all about how well you use all three to consistently communicate to your target audience over time.

The fourth most difficult part of this equation is figuring out where you will allocate your money. Once you have your brand, message, and strategy, you need to know where to spend the money to maximize the return and have a cost of acquisition that makes sense for your practice area.

Although the ratio formula will absolutely work, if you don't have the right marketing campaign mix, the marketing plan will be inefficient and the cost of your client acquisition will rise. We will discuss more about marketing campaigns later in this book.

The fifth and final challenge is knowing your earning period and your cash burn rate. Once you have your brand, message, and strategy and allocation correct, you need to know how long you can make the investment before you run out of cash and how long will it take to get your return on investment. This is especially true for contingency firms that tend to have longer time on desk actualization rates, and also need more people to manage the casework than the revenue that is being generated.

Strategize Your Spending Allocation

Once you've identified your marketing budget spend, the work is done. Kidding! Understanding your firm's economics and how they play into your overall marketing plan is only the foundation. Too many take their budget and throw it at one or two marketing channels or fail to evaluate whether the channels they've traditionally used are still working for them. Later in this book we will discuss campaign marketing versus channel marketing and how to build campaigns around your target audience so you can effectively and efficiently reach them without unnecessary expense. For now, conceptually, the second part of the formula of marketing spend is knowing the marketing allocation of your investments.

As a general rule, you should diversify the channels you'll allocate your marketing budget toward. My baseline marketing budget allocation is as follows:

- 5% - The Client Journey and Referrals
- 5% - Organic Social Media
- 10% - Search Engine Optimization (SEO)
- 10% - Pay Per Click Campaigns (PPC)
- 10%- Paid Social Media
- 60% - Brand Building

As I tell most of my clients, this is a guideline and not the gospel. Don't walk away from here and conclude that you have to use this as the end-all and be-all. Every practice is different, and some niche practices use very specific tried and true methods for marketing.

Recently, I was working with a firm that generated most of its business from direct mail. They would send one letter per month to a group of people who were in collections and needed debts resolved, and the next thing you know dozens of new leads came pouring in. That would probably never work for personal injury or business litigation. But that also doesn't mean you shouldn't use a newsletter strategy to keep your target market top of mind.

Not every practice area does well on social media. Being in the personal injury space, I can tell you that it is incredibly difficult to acquire clients on social media. If you want to have a social media strategy in personal injury, you may have to spend a lot more than a family law firm. In Chapter 9, I am going to take you on an in-depth look at social media and show you how you can use it for your own benefit and help you grow the practice you want.

Depending on your clientele and your practice area, these numbers will probably need to be adjusted, and that's okay. The most important step you can take is getting started. The most important area to get started in is in building your brand. If you are constantly in sales mode by buying leads through pay-per-click or lead generation, you will never develop the reputation and brand you need to ultimately reduce your cost of acquisition. As competition gets more fierce, acquiring cases through pay-per-click or lead generation becomes a much more taxing endeavor.

I remember about 15 years ago you would be able to sign up one case for less than $500. In today's market it could cost you more than $2000 to acquire that same case. The reason for this is the number of people who have entered the market space and have begun spending considerably more dollars in marketing and advertising to acquire cases. Although you may be able to afford the client acquisition today, this doesn't mean that the competition won't get so fierce that the profit margin on that same lead will disappear tomorrow.

Anytime you are singularly focused on one marketing strategy you are likely setting yourself up to lose a vital part of your revenue source in the event it falls apart. I have heard countless stories of people who have relied so heavily on one referral source that when the source died or discontinued the referral relationship, their revenues came crashing down. In later chapters, we'll discuss these different marketing channels in more detail, and you'll learn how best to utilize the marketing resources available to you.

Implement and Adjust

When I started working with entrepreneurs, I did not know how alike they were, especially the mindset of an entrepreneurial lawyer. One of the most surprising revelations was how quickly entrepreneurs can make one decision while simultaneously taking forever to make another. What I mean by this is that many entrepreneurs lead with their gut first, period, and if their gut is telling them to make a decision, they will instantly do it. But when the decision requires some level of calculation, such as building a marketing plan, or developing a business plan, they are much less likely to be able to pull the trigger and execute those plans.

When you start out on your 8 Figure Firm journey, you too may suffer from decision fatigue. Decision fatigue isn't uncommon among perfectionists, and perfectionism isn't uncommon among attorneys and law firm owners. That said, you can't delay the implementation of a new marketing strategy because you don't have 100 percent of the answers to questions like: is it better to start a blog, or is it better to secure more pay-per-clicks? You won't know some answers until after you've evaluated the analytics. At times, you will be wrong, but don't panic. We often learn more from getting something wrong than we do from getting something right. Never forget that a large part of marketing is testing, so many times you will be doing marketing that will not result in an immediate ROI. Many consultants in the legal industry space train law firm owners to only invest in things that produce a direct ROI. I think this is a faulty belief because anytime you do any activity with an expectation of an immediate and direct return on your investment, you are likely to miss out on the upside potential and opportunity of that activity.

I think a lot about the business in terms of a sports team. Many sports teams draft a potential professional athlete hoping that the athlete will later perform at a rate that generates enough revenue to cover their salary and create a profit. If sports teams relied on the direct return on investment strategy, it is likely that every time a professional athlete underperformed in a season they would have no choice but to release the player from the team. It's easy to see that this would be a mistake. In the professional world it takes time for even highly touted and drafted professionals to meet the expectations that these team owners have for them. Your marketing, your people, and your business are no different. There is a seasoning process that you must undergo to extract the value of the activity that you're engaged in.

When I hire new people, I never expect a direct return on investment. My expectation is that I can train them and mold them into something better and greater than the compensation that I'm paying for them today. Sometimes it works. Sometimes it does not work. But I cannot have the expectation that they will generate a return on my investment when they step into the building on day one.

Your marketing is no different. For each marketing channel there is a period you have to allow for that marketing investment to mature. The amount of time that you have to allow for that marketing investment to mature depends on the activity you're engaging in. Brand building is one of the longest investment strategies. But it is the strategy that can have the highest rate of return if executed properly. When I think about the success we have had at our law firm, a large part of it has been because of the tremendous investments we've made in brand building over the last five years. And so when you think about your marketing, I want you to think about an investment into a channel that requires a certain amount of time before the investment materializes. Your goal in this process is to continue to analyze when that investment should be doubled down on, redirected, or completely eliminated.

It may seem like an oversimplification, but the overarching themes of the 8 Figure Firm are implementation and adjustment. Step 1: implement your plan. Step 2: adjust as necessary. This is why a foundational understanding of law firm economics is so important. Profit, profitability, and revenue metrics provide insight that speaks to how successful the implementation of your marketing campaign is and where you may most need to adjust the plan.

Width and Depth?

As you continue marketing, you are looking at creating two different kinds of leads: 1. Width, and 2. Depth. Each is extremely important to the success of the other.

Most people spend most of their time trying to build depth, if they try at all. But most of your focus should be on building width so that you can grow the base from which you build depth.

The width of your business is built through marketing and advertising. This is when you expand your client base not by personal relationship building but rather through a proactive approach to reaching the client. Most law firms build their businesses by waiting for clients to come in the door. They believe that if they just do good work, people will eventually hear about them, and they will grow their business. To some extent this is true. The better the work you do, the better the reputation you will have. The better your reputation, the easier it is to get referrals. But what I have found in the last 20 years in this industry is that good work alone does not guarantee business growth and ultimately business success. And it absolutely does not provide a vehicle for you to scale. If your only goal is to grow in a slow manner, focusing all of your energies on referrals might work for you. But if you're reading this book, my assumption is that you want to scale your business and grow it faster and bigger than you've been able to grow it as of today. In order to take strides in your business so that your business is growing exponentially, not just through addition, you have to focus your efforts on reaching people who would not hear about you without an intentional and proactive approach to reaching out to them. In order for you to be seen by the people who need your services and your product, you have to be a good promoter of that great work.

Imagine having a restaurant with the best drink in the world or the best food in the world and relying on customers getting the word out for you to develop a reputation of how good it was. It would take decades to get the news to spread to another city or state. I travel a lot and I am always amazed when I find a local spot I've never heard of that has a two-hour wait. The reason the restaurant is so successful in its market but unknown outside of it is because it does not have an intentional and proactive marketing campaign.

A while back I took my nine year old son on a guys' trip to San Antonio. I went online and found several Mexican restaurants with good reviews. One of the restaurants had about 5000 reviews. I had not seen a single ad for them. They did not have a billboard, TV commercial, or radio commercial that I saw. Outside of the fact that I was searching for them by going online and looking at reviews, I would have never found them. Yet when I went to this particular restaurant there was a two-hour wait for a table for two. There were people waiting inside and lining up down the street. The food was OK. I don't know if I would have waited two hours the next time. What I do know is that this restaurant did not have a proactive and intentional approach to marketing its business. They had relied word of mouth advertising over decades. The restaurant had been in business for 30 years. Although this strategy worked for them, there's no guarantee that it will work for you. There's also no guarantee that you have the stamina to wait 30 years in order for your law firm to develop this sort of reputation.

If you want to grow fast and reach people outside of your current market and reputational reach, you have to put your name out into the world with a width-building marketing approach. It makes sense when you think about it. If a person has never heard of you, it is impossible for them to look you up online or call you. So, the focus on width is outreach. It is the activities we think of when we say advertising. We are trying to reach the unknown in quantities of scale. In a moment I will show you how width building plus depth building leads to exponential growth. But what is depth?

Depth is relationship building. These are your referrals. This is where most people start their law firm journey. They start telling all their friends and family about their new business venture and how they are working to help people. It goes back to my example above about the restaurant. Depth building is the word of mouth regarding your services. This can take an extremely long time because not only do you have to do great work, you have to create enough of a following that people refer other business to you. You can look up all kinds of studies that show that the amount of people who spread negativity about your business is far higher than the amount of people who spread positivity about your business.

I have met law firm owners who have worked for 25 to 30 years and their law firms have never grown past five or six employees and $1 million in revenue. And, man, they did they do great work. I can think of one of those lawyers just off the top of my head. He was brilliant. But at 65 years old, he had maybe 20 active cases, lots of debt, and no physical health to continue his business. What a terrible way to end your legal career.

Nevertheless, depth building is absolutely necessary to the growth of your business. The best depth building happens when you commit to it with intentionality. At 8 Figure Firm, we call depth building the Signature Client Journey. This is a series of communications through text, email, and phone calls coupled with video delivery, gift-giving and asking for referrals that, if you do it correctly, will lead to amazing success in your business. But it must be intentional. Here's the thing. Your clients are also on a journey, whether you know it or not. The real issue is whether the journey they are on is the journey you want them to be on. Is it the journey that best represents your business? Is it the journey that satisfies you the most for the way you treat the client?

To grow a big law business, you cannot leave things up to chance. That is a surefire way to destroy your law firm's growth prospect and ensure that you are always a small law firm. If you want to play guessing games with your money, go to Vegas. If you want consistent financial growth, work to understand your law firm's economic equation.

Width building and debt building work in conjunction, and both of them are necessary. And the more intentional you are about both, the more likely it is that you will develop a business with exponential growth. The way these two concepts work together can best be described by showing you two sets of law firms.

Assume law firm one starts on day one and spends no money on width building and no money on outreach. Two or three days into opening their doors one new client signs with them. The client is relatively satisfied and has no complaints about the quality of work or the representation. While the first client is being represented, the law firm receives another client two or three days later. And every two or three days after that, a new lead comes in. This law firm is very lucky. Because in a matter of 30 days this law firm has managed to acquire 10 new clients. This is a dream come true.

Nevertheless, this law firm does not have an intentional width-building strategy and must rely on the 10 new clients to continue to spread the word of mouth. And as you may already know, it's much less likely that you will refer people to a good business than complain about a bad business. So two out of these 10 refer someone new, and in the very next month the law firm is fortunate enough to sign 10 more new clients plus the two that were referred by the existing clients. Now the law firm has signed 12 total clients. The next month the same thing happens. Twenty percent of the clients produce one referral each. In the third month three new clients hire the firm plus 10 additional clients. After three months the law firm has signed 10, 12, and 13 clients each month.

In contrast, law firm number two decides to spend money on width building. They received a loan from the SBA to start their firm. (I know this is hard to get but it's for illustrative purposes. Imagine the money came from any source you deem realistic). They received $30,000. They studied their market, and they understand that the market commands a $500 cost of acquisition. They know that with $5,000 they would be able to generate 10 new clients. They decided to go out and build depth just like the first law firm. But they spend half of the money that they received on client acquisition and the other half on operations.

In month one the second law firm generates 10 new clients just like the first law firm, but because of the width building strategy they also acquire 10 new clients. Law firm number two also does great work. They now have 20 new clients in month one. Twenty percent of these clients refer a client to them. The law firm decides to invest the second half of the loan and acquires 10 new clients, an additional four new clients from referrals, and 10 new clients from width building. In month two, law firm number two has now been hired by 24 new clients. Month three rolls around and the same thing happens. Twenty percent referral clients come in and an investment is made into the acquisition of new clients. In month three, the law firm signs 29 new clients.

In scenario one the law firm signed 35 new clients in the first three months of business. In the second scenario the law firm signs 55 clients in the first three months of business. The difference in client acquisition leads to an opportunity to reinvest an additional $200,000 in revenue back into the business.

This is why simultaneous width and depth building is critical to your success if you want to grow and scale a fast organization.

The good news in all of this is that people are extremely predictable. What this means is that this formula for marketing will create a level of predictability in your firm if you commit to the formula for the requisite period of time. How much time? It's different for everyone.

Do not underestimate the compounding effect that consistency brings over time.

The time component is where everyone gets frustrated. Because the amount of time it may take me to build my business may not be the amount of time it takes you, even using the same strategies. I wish this wasn't the case. But every brand has its own journey. This could be because of the brand appeal, the message, the timing of your marketing, and many other things which we will cover in detail in this book. The key to seeing success is to stay focused on your strategy and continue to refine the message so that you maximize your desired outcome. Do not underestimate the compounding effect that consistency brings over time.

In order for you to understand the strategies that I will share in this book, you have to first understand and accept the economics of marketing. And the economics of marketing are not well-understood in the legal industry. In many other industries there are known marketing strategies that have helped companies succeed at a high level. But for whatever reason, the legal industry has been very slow to implement many of these strategies. After many years of learning and reading, I have developed a strategy that will create incredible momentum in your business and establish a great level of predictability for the future of your organization.

Here is the full formula. We will go into each in more depth for the rest of this book:

1. **Vision + Mission + Values + Standards + USP + Goals = Message**

2. **You + Message = Brand**

3. **Brand X 25% of last year's revenues spent in marketing = Leads**

4. **Leads + Sales = Conversions**

5. **Conversions + People + Client Retention = Revenue**

6. **Revenues – Payroll/Overhead = Profit**

7. **Formula implemented Consistently = Predictable Law Business**

CHAPTER 2

THE 6 ESSENTIALS OF A MESSAGE

"When marketing is not grounded in a foundation of authentic messaging with authority, integrity and ability, it can end up costing worlds more, saying worlds less and sounding the same as so many others."

Loren Weisman

Have you ever wondered how brands can sell handbags for $3,000 or more, or how shoe companies can sell shoes for $1,000 or more, and yet some lawyers have difficulty selling life-changing services for $2,000 or$5,000? The answer is in the message.

The other day I was walking through the mall, and I passed by a section where all of the luxury stores are located. Most of them had lines but none with longer lines than Louis Vuitton. That line had zigzags, two employees outside checking people in, and two security officers. People waited up to an hour just to get into the store to buy a handbag or a duffle bag for $2,000 to $10,000.

How did they create this sort of buzz? How do they command this sort of loyalty? In that same line, I saw people taking selfies with the store in the background to show people on social media.

When you look up LV's mission and vision, you quickly find they claim "To be the most prestigious and desirable luxury goods company." It appears that they are executing that mission and message.

Your message is what you communicate to the world. It is the promise you make to your ideal client. A message is a theme you want the world to know about your law firm. Every law firm has a different message, even if they practice in the same geographic location or sell the same law service.

If you have a weak message, you will have a weak following. If you have a strong message, you will have a strong following. A message is something that can cut through the noise of the competition and solidify your place in the market as the go-to source for legal services. Before you start any marketing campaign, you must have your message ready to go. All of your marketing channels must be message-aligned so that you can maximize the outcome of your spend and not create inefficient marketing.

But how do you create a message that is impactful and unique? Below I will walk you through the 10 essentials of your message and how to construct one to give you the leading edge in the marketplace.

1. Define Your Vision

Without a vision it is impossible to take your business to the next level. I know some of you want to look past this part of the book. But I want you to hold on just one minute and entertain me as I explain how your vision will outline your eventual message for your marketing.

When my business partner and I started working together we had the blessing of meeting one of the premier hotel industry leaders in the world. He was the former CEO of the Ritz Carlton. He was willing to share with us the secret to building a great business. The first thing he told us was that we had to have a vision so big that it would take a lifetime to achieve. He said that building a great business required that the vision would be good for us, for the employees, for the clients, and for the community. At the time, we couldn't understand what that meant in the legal industry. What is that vision? What did it look like? To us, every law firm had the same vision. They had the same reason for existing. We could not think of anything that would distinguish us from other law firms in our industry. But what we realized after much thought and personal search is that our vision was the only thing that differentiated us from other law firms. Our vision came from Our Calling.

In the same way, your vision will come from your calling. Understanding this, we worked tirelessly for weeks to find the words that would capture the vision we were trying to achieve. If this was so important, we thought, we should put as much effort as we possibly could into figuring out the words that would guide our business. We spent almost one month putting together the vision of our business. In the end all we had was one sentence, but that sentence was enough to drive double-digit growth in a short period of time.

What Vision Is Not

This vision is not a mission statement.

Your mission statement describes <u>who you are as a business</u> and what you are going to do to accomplish your vision.

Your vision statement declares <u>what you will do as a business</u>.

Your mission articulates what your firm does, but your vision outlines where your firm is going. Your mission statement lives in the present tense while your vision statement forecasts the future.

For my company, 8 Figure Firm, our vision is "To be the leading authority in law firm building." This will take a lifetime to achieve, and I may never achieve it. It informs what I want to do in the future. It doesn't, however, inform how I will actually get there. That answer lies in the mission.

I know what you are reading here may sound very different from what you have heard and read before. When you go online, you will hear a lot about what the vision and mission is for your business. Many of those opinions will say that the vision and mission are the same thing. But I want you to think of the vision and the mission in a different way. Your vision informs only where the business is going in the future, even if that vision is written in an abstract way.

Your vision is not a vague hope or dream. It's a picture of a real result that will be obtained by your efforts.

Here's another key differentiator between *mission* and *vision*: While your mission statement is important for everyone who interacts with your firm, you're primarily making it public for your clients—the people with whom you will do business. Your vision statement is primarily for your team, the people who will work with you. Your clients don't necessarily need to know your vision statement, but they will absolutely be impacted by it because it will be the guiding light of the business.

In other words—your *mission statement faces outward*, and your *vision statement faces inward.*

Your vision is not a vague hope or dream. It's a picture of a real result that will be obtained by your efforts—if you put in the work, of course. It's a picture of the business you want that is so clear that you can almost experience it today even though you have not yet achieved it.

Writing the 8 Figure Vision

When I decided to build 8 Figure Firm Consulting, I knew I needed a vision because that is what propelled us in building Bader Scott Injury Lawyers. When I sat down and thought about the vision for 8 Figure Firm, I asked myself, "What is the legacy that I want to leave if I ever leave the company?" After thinking about it carefully, I realized I wanted to help people maximize their calling in life. I had already developed a personal vision statement: to lead a life of significance. But how was I going to lead a life of significance in my new business venture? The answer came in the form of being the leading authority in law firm building.

As I contemplated what this meant, I thought to myself, "if I could be the leading authority in law firm building, maybe, just maybe, I could change the world and thus lead a life of significance."

But it would take a lifetime to achieve this. There's no way that in a year or two or even three I would become the leading authority in law firm building. At least that's what I believed. There were already so many people in the legal space teaching others how to learn and grow their own law firms. The thing that made me unique was that I had actually built an eight-figure firm. I thought that would be a huge selling point in developing my own business. But I knew if I wanted to be the leading authority in law firm building, it would take me a lifetime. It would take me rallying other people who shared the same vision of helping people across the country maximize their potential.

As you can see, your vision for your company is probably not so different than the vision you have for your life. Regardless of your practice area, your vision for your life will generally be different from the vision that your competitor has for their life. That makes your law firm unique. Now you must figure out a way to communicate this vision.

Why Do You Need a Compelling Vision Statement?

You need a vision statement because without one, you as an owner do not really know what you are trying to accomplish. And no, helping people and making money is not a vision statement that people can truly rally behind. A vision statement geared around "helping people" is too cliché to be believed, and one geared around "making money" is too shallow to inspire. The vision has to be something that when people hear it, they genuinely feel a sense of "wow" and are inspired to come on board and work with you. I have found that visions that revolve around being the biggest and best tend to encourage high achievers to come work for you. The vision then serves to inspire the work product of your top performers as well.

You may only have employees right now—heck, you may not have any employees—and you may be thinking, why do I need a vision for my business? Simple. Without a vision, you will not be able to experience fast and high growth because no one will know why your business is even worth it. And, yes, this is true even for a law firm.

Having a clear vision that employees can rally behind will create incredible engagement in your organization, enhance the culture, and give direction to the leadership.

Joseph Folkman, a behavioral statistician focused on leadership development, compiled some eye-opening research on this topic and published his findings in Forbes. In studying the responses of 50,000 employees, Folkman's team discovered that employees who didn't find their company's vision meaningful had engagement scores of only 16 percent. Conversely, when employees could get behind the company vision, engagement rose to 68 percent. This reveals a direct correlation between how compelling a company's vision statement is and how committed its employees are to following it.

As you know, employee engagement is tied to high efficiency in your organization, better culture, and less turnover, all things that are incredibly important to having a law business instead of merely a law firm.

Now, you don't have to go too deep into the math to see the ramifications here. If your employees are only 16 percent interested in your vision, how much help do you really think they are going to be in fulfilling that vision? Answer: Not much. And how likely do you think it will be that you can build a fast-growing organization with only a 16 percent engagement score? Again: Not likely.

With that sort of engagement, you're going to be doing most of the heavy lifting, and you might even find yourself dragging along some extra dead weight. On the other hand, if you've got an engagement level of 68 percent or more, the vision is practically going to fulfill itself—in fact, you may find yourself running to catch up! That is what I experienced both in the law firm and in 8 Figure Firm Consulting. The vision has driven me to wild success, all because of the direction that it has provided.

Part of the reason that many law firm owners can't get their business off the ground and into explosive growth mode is that they either do not have a vision or the vision is not compelling enough to inspire employees to see it through. And part of the reason most businesses do not write down their vision is that they do not see a direct return on investment. In business, direct return on investment is not always attainable. Sometimes the investment is only one piece of what you must do so that the other pieces of your business will create the return. The vision is that piece.

In my first firm, we did not have a vision at all. We had a lot of employees working their nine to five every day without very much effort outside of that. I became a nine to fiver myself. After 10 years of working in the firm, I was not striving for anything more than what we already had. There was no energy. There was no engagement or enthusiasm. People did not work late at night or on weekends. (I'm not saying this has to happen, but when you have a fast-growing organization with high achievers, this will be one of the indicators). This lack of achievement created an emptiness in my spirit. I wanted more for myself and the law firm, but I did not have any direction.

Fast forward to my new firm, and you find that our compelling vision has created over three dozen fully committed leaders. We have 40 leaders who are on fire to help us generate fast growth in the company. We have leaders who put in the time and effort, leaders who we trust so much that I was able to be gone from my firm for 12 days without any contact and the business kept thriving. Today, I only need to put in three hours per week for my firm to continue functioning at a high level. Every quarter the firm continues to grow in both new clients and revenue without my involvement in the sales or production of the business. All of this is because the leaders know and understand the vision of the business. If you are calling BS on this claim, I want you to remember that this is only essential number one. We still have 10 more essentials that will create the foundation for your message.

Characteristics of a Solid Vision Statement

Your vision statement should absolutely be forward-looking. It should articulate a big vision, one that requires more than just your effort to attain. You will see the most impact if your statement meets the following characteristics:

- *It is concise.* The vision statement should be short and sweet. You can create a longer, expanded version of it for yourself and your key players if you wish, but try to limit your forward-facing version to one or two sentences. The vision statement should be no more than 20 words long. My vision was eight words. There is plenty of literature that will disagree with this point. However, I believe that if your vision statement is concise, it will be easier for people to remember and digest the content than if it is a paragraph long with complicated sections.

- *It is memorable.* Your team should be able to commit it to memory and repeat it verbatim. It does not have to be catchy. It just needs to be something that people can remember without much effort. I love the vision statement for Disney: "to be one of the world's leading producers and providers of entertainment and information." Easy to remember.

- *It is emotional, inspirational, and motivational.* Does this vision evoke a response? Does it inspire people to act? The best vision statements give people a sense of belonging and a sense of pride. Vision statements almost force the reader to want to be a part of the business.

- *It is future-oriented.* It describes what your law firm aspires to accomplish over time. It is something that looks to the future. Like Disney's, it will take a lifetime to accomplish.

- *It's ambitious while avoiding fluff and superlative language.* Your vision can project challenging goals, but superlatives can generate a lack of faith. Terms like "industry leader" or "prominent" are fine, but "world domination"—not so much. Make sure the words match what you actually want to be known for and not simply something you think sounds great to other people.

Examples of Compelling Vision Statements

Note how all these examples face the future, saying what the company aspires to do, not who they are:

- "Our vision is to create a better everyday life for many people." —IKEA (Ambitious, yet general—and manages expectations.)

- "To be Earth's most customer-centric company, where customers can find and discover anything they might want to buy online, and endeavors to offer its customers the lowest possible prices."—Amazon (Look at what they've done since they started—this vision statement almost seems prophetic, it's so accurate.)

- "A world without Alzheimer's disease."—Alzheimer's Association (Super short, yet it leaves no doubt what the organization is aiming toward.)

- "A computer on every desk and in every home." — original vision for Microsoft

- "Create economic opportunity for every member of the global workforce." —LinkedIn

You may be thinking you do not have a big enough business for a vision statement, but you would be completely wrong. Without a vision, a true sense of direction for your business, you will never have a law firm that runs completely on its own with engaged employees creating tremendous value in the world.

The first essential to your message and explosive growth is the vision of your law firm.

2. What Is Your Actionable Mission?

Essential number two is the actionable mission. With a clear and concise vision in mind, you are now ready to start figuring out how you are going to accomplish this big vision. This is where the mission statement comes into play. The mission statement will tell your team and the world what you need to do each day so that you can eventually accomplish the vision of the organization.

In essential one, I explained that the 8 Figure vision was to become the leading authority in law firm building. How would this be achieved? That's what the mission will answer.

What Is a Mission Statement?

A well-crafted mission statement serves as a compass of sorts, helping you clarify your priorities and guiding your decisions as a business. It's especially important for a law firm to have a mission statement because of the sheer number of possible directions a law practice can take. A mission statement helps you stay grounded and focused on the projects and clients that truly matter to you and your firm. The mission will also inform how your law firm will achieve the high-level success your vision statement has laid out.

Difference Between a Mission Statement and a Vision Statement

Many people erroneously use the terms *vision statement* and *mission statement* interchangeably. In truth, they work together, but they are not the same thing. The best way we've found to differentiate between the two is that a *mission statement describes how you will achieve your vision*, while a *vision statement declares what you want your business to achieve*.

Here's another way to think of it:

- A *vision statement* answers the question *What?*
- A *mission statement* answers the question *How?*

Again, this may be different than what you have heard before; if it is, good! That means it is novel. If it isn't, then also good because that means you just need to implement. I use vision and mission in a very specific ways. If you do not craft your vision and mission in this way, it is likely that your vision and mission will be known by no one and will not provide any benefit to your firm.

When I ask most law firm owners what their vision is, many times they have to pull out a dusty computer they no longer use to find the document where they wrote the vision and mission statements four, five, or even 10 years ago. That is not what we want when we are working to craft your message. We want a vision and mission that are alive and used daily within the organization and outside of its four walls.

Here is how the interplay should be when using a simple vision and mission statements.

- Vision: To be the state's leading authority in family law.

- Mission: We lead the state in family law by providing access to the toughest legal representation, employing the most compassionate legal staff, and delivering the highest level of customer service.

That seems simple. But as you can see, you have a big vision of being the leading authority in your state. It could take a lifetime to accomplish that vision. It is a vision that will inspire staff and help you hire the right people for your organization. The mission will give context on how you will become the leading authority.

The mission says how you will accomplish becoming the leading authority. Everyone from the people who clean your offices, to the marketing team, to the lawyers, and to the families of the employees will know how you will accomplish the vision of the organization. This clarity will help you define your key performance indicators, acquire talent, and even let people go if necessary.

Anatomy of a Good Mission Statement

Opinions about what should go into a good mission statement vary widely—ironically, if you take all the opinions into account, you'll have written a book when you're done. That defeats the purpose. From my perspective, the best way to keep your mission statement focused is simply to make sure it touches on the following three points:

1. *What* you do;

2. *How* you do it; and

3. *Who* you do it for.

Let's explore these three in more detail as they pertain to your law firm. Some questions to ask yourself:

1. *What you do.* Of all the different ways you could practice law, what specific concentration(s) will you focus on? What will your firm be known for in your community? In my law firm, we do injury law. Part of the mission statement therefore needed to touch on how we solve the problems our clients face. If you read my law firm's mission statement, you will find that we provide access to the highest-level medical and legal services. That is one part of the mission.

2. *How you do it.* What in the way you approach your clients or your cases will differentiate you from other law firms? What do you do that gives you a competitive advantage? In my firm's mission statement, we want to make the person complete and whole. We provide the access I mentioned in question one to make the person whole physically, emotionally, and financially. This is unique because not every personal injury firm has this goal in mind. Having this goal provides context for how we will engage in the representation with clients.

3. *Who do you do it for.* Don't just consider your clients in this case, but your employees as well. Your mission statement will inform your company culture. Who is your ideal client? Who is your ideal teammate? How will you treat both your clients and employees? What value do they each bring to your company?

When you put my law firm mission statement together, you get: "We empower the injured (Who) by providing access to the highest level medical and legal services (What) to heal the client physically, emotionally, and financially (How)."

Here's the real challenge you face when writing your mission statement: You have to take the stuff you're most passionate about (which most of us can talk about for hours) and boil it down into one to three sentences that sum up your company's entire purpose. Your mission can't be a long

46

dissertation because your goal is to win people over to your purpose, and they'll lose focus if it rambles. For that reason, crafting a compelling mission statement often requires a great deal of thought, and you might go through many iterations before you decide on the right version.

I would plan on writing and then rewriting your mission statement a dozen times or so. Shop it around and see what variations resonate the most with people. Ask your employees what they think about the mission statements you have drafted. If you have some A+ ideal clients who were satisfied with your services, invite them in to hear about your new mission and see what they think.

The success of this group-think project will depend on how you phrase the ask. Do not ask these audiences if they like it. Ask them to help you make it more concise or clear. Ask them to help you see where it needs work. Get honest feedback and not just idle praise. This will help your mission statement come to life.

Why Your Mission Statement Matters

Let's say you have no trouble at all describing why you started your law firm. You're so in tune with your passions that you can talk about them in your sleep. You now have this super catchy, big, audacious mission statement ready to hit the market on a moment's notice. So, *why do you need to write down a mission statement? Why go to the trouble of writing out a mission statement when it's all so clear in your head and you already have the other stuff?*

You just answered the question: It's all in your head.

You see, you are not the only one who needs to know what you're about. You're not doing this thing in a vacuum. In fact, there are at least three different categories of people who really need you to write down this mission statement so they, too, can get behind it fully. They are:

- *Your team.* We'll get into effective team-building later, but as a starting point—your team can't truly function as an extension of you unless they can commit the mission to memory and own it for themselves. The mission is how they will achieve the vision. Your team needs to have some direction on how you, as the owner of the firm, want the vision to be accomplished. There are so many strategies for building a business; your team needs to know your particular strategy.

- *Your clients.* A clearly defined mission statement helps your current and future clients understand the value they're getting when they decide to work with you. Why should a client hire your law firm? Easy: your mission statement. Your mission statement will guide your law firm to provide the legal representation every single client deserves.

- *Yourself.* Yes, even *you* need to see your mission statement in writing, even if you think you don't. At some point on this journey, you're going to face some challenges or be tempted to take some left turns. You might start losing sight of why you started this firm— or indeed, why you chose to be a lawyer in the first place. You need to *externalize* your mission statement so you can always come back to it and find your compass again. Your mission statement will help keep you grounded and focused.

We're not saying it will be easy to find the right combination of words to express your mission. Quite the opposite. But if you commit to the process until you've got it right, you'll never regret doing so. It will set your firm on a good foundation and help you rally the right people around you to put feet to your vision.

And if things get rough or you lose your way, it might just be the thing that saves your business.

Tying Mission and Vision Together

One thought before leaving this topic. We've spent a lot of time differentiating between *mission statement* and *vision statement* because so many people confuse the two. But when you put in the effort to craft both statements, they will ideally complement each other. Your vision will line up with your mission, and your stated goal will be in character with who you've said you are as a company. This is why the mission statement is not enough on its own.

I started this section by outlining the vision for 8 Figure Firm: to be the leading authority in law firm building. The actionable mission is "To help 100 law firms experience 8 Figures in predictable revenue." I believe if we can execute the mission, we will one day reach the vision of being the leading authority in law firm building. And even if we do not become this, we will absolutely change the world.

Essential number two for your message is to craft a mission statement that is clear and concise. Make sure it is a guiding statement putting feet to the vision. Then work to execute that mission statement day after day.

3. What Will You Stand For?

Have you ever been playing a board game with a group of people when, just for fun, someone randomly decides to change or ignore all the rules? It can be hilarious at first (being several drinks into the evening definitely helps), but after a few minutes, everything devolves into chaos, and the game is no longer fun. Usually, the game ends soon after this moment.

Why? Simple: Every game, competition, race, or battle requires a set of rules in order to have value. If you have no rules, you have no clear path to victory—and therefore no way to determine a winner. So, what's the point of playing?

Have you ever had an altercation with your significant other, and one of you says or does something that is obviously "below the belt"? It changes the whole nature of the conflict. Even though the rules of engagement may be unspoken, you both know instinctively when those rules have been broken. It may end the fight. It also may end the relationship.

These two scenarios illustrate the idea behind our next essential. Once you've created a vision and mission statement, you need to identify a set of core values for your business. The core values are not just something you hang up on the wall for people to see when they walk in. The core values represent the heartbeat of the ownership. These are the rules under which the business will operate. This is what the employees will feel and experience as part of your growing culture. Ultimately this will form part of the message that you will communicate to the world.

This task is probably the most intuitive one you will undertake in laying the groundwork for your law firm—because all you're going to do is identify something that is already in place. You don't need to "come up with" core values. Core values are innate to who you are as an owner. You already have core values. We all operate by core values even when we haven't specifically named what they are. Your challenge isn't to decide on some core values for your firm, but simply to identify and verbalize them. It's a journey of discovery.

You must put the core values in writing so that all who work with you, from your employees to your vendors, know for what you stand.

What Are Core Values?

Core values are basically a set of beliefs or ideas about what is most important to you, whether personally or corporately. They serve as the guiding principles behind every decision you make. Think of them as the internal "rules of engagement" for your law firm—the rules that give value to the game and provide meaning to your future success. Core values inform both your mission and vision because they set the boundaries for what you *will* and *will not* do to accomplish your goals. They also play a key role in what kinds of goals you decide to go after in the first place.

I love quoting the movie *The Godfather*. When I was growing up, my dad used to quote the guiding principles of this mob family. As I grew older, I realized what these quotes actually were. They were the core values of the family business. Today, some of these quotes even guide how I think about the business, and I even say them to my business partner from time to time. They are not my core values—they're just fun to use in certain contexts.

Here is some of my favorites from the movie:

1. Never hate your enemies. It affects your judgment.

2. Never let anyone know what you are thinking.

3. Don't ever take sides with anyone against the family.

4. Don't ever ask me about my business.

There were a lot of "don'ts" coming from Michael Corleone. But these core values informed the way the business was going to be run. It was the message that was communicated to the team and to those outside of the family. And everyone was subject to the rules of the game. If you got out of line, you would be subject to the discipline of the family.

Just for clarity, I am not suggesting you run your organization like a mob boss. The takeaway is that whether you have the core values written down or not, you are operating by them. And the best way to make sure your organization adheres to the boundary and the rules is to write them down and communicate them often.

Perhaps by now, you're starting to see a method to my madness—a logical progression for your message:

1. If your vision statement describes what you plan to achieve, and

2. Your mission statement describes how you will achieve it, then

3. Your core values provide the compass for getting there.

Using your core values, you will develop a plan for hiring and acquiring talent consistent with your values. Imagine having a core value of hard work and you hire someone who likes to work only nine to five and take long leisurely lunches? What if one of your core values is togetherness and you hire an employee who wants to work alone at home? How would it work in these scenarios? I have the answer.... it wouldn't.

Core values will define the boundaries of your business along with the qualities of the person you are looking for. In essence, you will be looking for people just like you. People who have the same values that you have. That is what I call having good culture. When you have an organization that functions along with the heartbeat of the owner and the employees love what they do, synergy will emerge.

How Core Values Are Expressed

Most companies define their core values as a list of single words or short phrases. They may be expressed as simple bullet points, sometimes followed by a brief explanation of why each particular value matters to them. These values won't always be directly related to your business dealings or your customer relationships, but they will always inform your worldview at some level because they represent who you are at your core. If you know anything about Patagonia, for example, you know that environmental sustainability is one of their core values. You can't separate the brand from the cause, in fact. As core values go, it's not completely business-related, but it informs every choice they make as a business.

The same goes for the message. The core values may not be explicitly stated in the message, but they will inform the way the message is crafted and your ideal client will be aware of the rules of engagement with your firm.

Unlike your mission and vision statements, when you craft your list of core values, you don't have to worry too much about length. Each value may be a simple word or phrase, but you're not necessarily trying to get everything down to a single sentence like the previous steps. Just bear in mind that you want your list to be easy to remember, so the more core values you have, the more challenging it may be to recall them all.

Examples of Core Values

To give you an idea of what core values might look like, below is a small sampling of values many businesses have adopted. See if you relate to any of these:

- Loyalty
- Faith
- Integrity
- Excellence
- Honesty
- Innovation
- Customer first
- Motivation
- Efficiency
- People-centered
- Creativity
- Social responsibility
- Sense of humor
- Community

- Optimism
- Environmentalism
- Respect
- Perseverance
- Persistence
- Service-oriented
- Positivity
- Reliability
- Truth
- Kindness

When my business partner and I crafted our core values for our law firm we first did the single words. We came up with the acronym G.R.O.W.T.H.: Growth, Gratitude, Respect, Open Heart, Winning, Trust, and Humility. It was easy to remember and easy to communicate.

Later we transitioned to short phrases that we thought would better serve our business.

- Clients Come First
- Respect without Exception
- Lead with Heart, Lead through Service
- See It, Own It, Do It
- Make Today Better than Yesterday

Using either individual words or short phrases is fine so long as it reflects who you are as an owner.

In both instances, our core values were a reflection of who we were as owners and what we represented. If our core value was "clients come first," everything about our business needed to communicate this value. For this reason, we created a client lounge, did mandatory customer service training for our employees, and even developed a no-voicemail policy. All of this was then communicated as part of our message to the community both inside and outside of the organization.

Things to Consider When Making Your List

Feel free to brainstorm and be creative when figuring out your core values, either alone or with trusted members of your team. Ultimately the values should come from you because you will be the one to live with them when your employees are long gone. But having a group of people to bounce ideas off can be helpful. Once you have a nice list of possible values, review the items one by one to decide whether each value carries enough importance to be part of your company canon. During this stage, keep the following tips in mind:

- *Reflect on each core value in the context of your law firm's culture.* Don't adopt a core value just because it's popular or "a good idea." Make sure that value is genuinely part of your key motivation as a firm owner. Remember, the idea is to identify the core values which are *already there because in essence they are a part of who you are.* You can't be and do *all* the good things, so just decide which good things matter most to you.

- *There's no set guideline for how many core values you should have.* However, each core value needs to be authentic to your organization. If you have too few, your list will not reflect accurately who you are. If you have too many, people will not be able to fit into that mold. You need to select the absolute CORE essence of who you are. As amazing as you think you may be, you do not have at your core all things. I would say to narrow your core values to no more than eight but preferably five total. These will be the core characteristics of who you are.

- *Your company values should be a reflection of your personal values—they may even be the same.* As a lawyer and a small business owner, your personal motivations can (and probably should) be part of what drives your firm, as well. If you value hard work personally, your business should reflect that.

Since we're going on the premise that these core values already exist and that they drive your actions, is it possible to function by these values without having to write them out? In theory, sure—if you plan to be a one-person company. To you, these values may operate as pure instinct. But to go where you need to go as a company, you're going to need a *team*, and your team can't abide by the company's core values unless they know what they are. These are your law firm's rules of engagement. Write them down and make them plain. Make sure that they govern how people in your organization operate.

4. Setting Your Service Standards

Essential number four is having minimum service standards. Up to this point, we've been dealing in generalizations and abstract ideals—basic building blocks that help form the foundation for all you will accomplish in your law firm. Now, it's time to get specific. With this step, you're going to create a set of service standards that will serve as a uniform guide for every client interaction you and your team will have going forward.

As the saying goes, when chopping down a tree, be sure to sharpen the axe first. This is what you are doing. You are sharpening the axe. It may feel that the tree is not coming down because while you are sharpening the axe, you don't see any progress. But once you get started chopping, the result will be exponential. In the same way, when you do your vision, mission, and values process, it may seem like nothing is happening. But if you get the business very sharp, when you start marketing and representing clients, you will see an explosion of growth in your business like you could have never imagined.

You can see by now that these steps are progressive, so let's put this one in context:

- If your **vision statement** describes *what you plan to achieve,* and

- Your **mission statement** describes *how you will achieve it,* and

- Your **core values** provide the *compass for getting there,* then

- Your **service standards** will *flesh out specific guidelines and rules* for customer interactions based on your vision, mission, and values.

The first three steps sketch out a general picture of how you want your law firm to function in the world. With this fourth step, you're describing what that function will look like in real life—specifically, how it will look when it comes to your client relationships.

Purpose of the Service Standards

We'll say this probably several times in the course of this book, and we say it repeatedly to the attorneys we work with directly: *Your clients are your lifeblood.* Without clients you do not have a business. No matter how much you know about the law, no matter how passionate you are about helping people, no matter how driven you are to build a great law firm, if you don't have clients, your law firm is nothing but an idea. All the groundwork you've laid so far leads to this one point: *How your law firm is going to interact with clients.* How will you attract clients? How will you serve them? How will you treat them once you have them? What will you do to keep them? How will you provide a service that is different from the competition and noticeable in every interaction with your team? How will your firm set itself apart? How will you communicate this value directly to the client?

When my business partner and I thought about the service standards we wanted for our firm, we first listed all of the things we did not want. We did not want clients waiting on the phone for long periods of time. We did not want client calls going to the black hole of voicemail. We did not want attorneys not speaking to their clients at the beginning of the case. We did not want clients to not feel welcome in our office.

Therefore, as we crafted our service standards, we had some of the do-not-wants in mind. Some of our service standards address these issues directly, such as:

1. Call times at reception should be less than two minutes

2. No-voicemail policy

3. Attorneys must speak to clients within 48 hours of hire

4. Say hello to clients if you walk into the lobby

These service standards became the minimum expectation for all of our staff and lawyers. This was the message we wanted to communicate to the world.

Get Everyone on the Same Page

Again, if your law firm were just about you, you might instinctively know how you want your customers to be treated. I've heard this so many times from law firm owners: "When I represented clients and was the only attorney in the firm, every client knew my name. Every client had my phone number. No one ever terminated my services. Every client was happy. I always got good reviews."

That sounds great, but have you communicated to your team and your other lawyers how you expect them to behave with clients? Have you taught them what you did to have such a high satisfaction rate? Have you shown the team how to attract and retain great clients? How to treat each person as an individual and not just a number? Just because you did it exceptionally well does not mean that everyone else knows how to do it that way, especially if you have invested no time in showing them how to do it.

I know what you are thinking: it's common sense. They should all already know. But nothing is common sense because we all have different life experiences. My philosophy has always been to expect that your team knows nothing—but don't treat them that way. In this way, you are always looking to educate them. If they don't need education, you have lost nothing in the process.

What you believe is common sense will not be so for your team because your team will never be able to care about your business as much as you care about your business. They have likely not had the same life experience or the same training as you. So, they likely will not know what you believe is common sense when it comes to dealing with clients. What you believe to be common sense was probably a foreign concept to you at one point.

Even if everyone you hire is firmly behind your vision, mission, and values (as we all hope they would be), that doesn't mean every employee will interpret those values the same way when they deal with customers. Your service standards create a uniform policy that removes the ambiguity and tells your team *exactly* what it looks like for a client to interact with your law firm. The goal here is that every client gets the *same quality experience* when working with your firm, no matter which team member they happen to be dealing with on any given day. In fact, many firms view their service standards as part of their employee handbook, and some even have their employees sign it as part of their onboarding process.

In addition to having every employee on the same page as to how to treat a client, your service standards will help write the message of your law firm, which will in turn help you cut through the noise of the competition.

Characteristics of Well-Written Service Standards

Your service standards should be written in such a way that your team can fully understand and execute them. To that end, each standard should be:

- *Specific, not vague.* "Make the client happy" is too ambiguous. "Treat each customer with kindness and respect" is better. Even more specific could be the way Chick-Fil-A trains their staff to say, "my pleasure" after a customer interaction.

- *Measurable.* Associate the standard with some sort of metric so everyone can tell if it's being met. (BAD: "Answer every email as quickly as possible." GOOD: "Answer every email within 24 hours.") Employees should know what "good customer service" looks like and sounds like. Do not leave it up to chance. In our firm we have a no-voicemail policy and return all calls by the end of the day. We do not always succeed, but there is no ambiguity as to what the standard is.

- *Consistent with company culture.* Try to choose standards that can be tied to your vision, mission, and values in some way. One of our values is "Clients come first." This is the reason we have a no-voicemail standard. When a client calls and you are doing something else, you take the client call because clients come first.

- *Accessible.* Service standards may challenge your employees to do better, but should not be so lofty that the standard feels unattainable. Also, with regard to the standards as a whole, try to maintain a sense of balance and don't overwhelm employees with so many rules that they feel your overall expectations are impossible to meet. Make sure the standard is the floor, not the ceiling. If the standard is too hard to meet, it will not be met and the team will become discouraged. Also, try to keep the standards to less than 12.

Should You Post Your Service Standards for Your Clients?

Use your own best judgment here. Service standards are designed largely as a *guide for employees* for the *benefit of your clients.* The good thing about posting them publicly is that it keeps you and your team accountable. The bad thing: It keeps you and your team accountable. In other words, if you fall short of the standards—even if you tried your hardest—your clients will definitely let you know. At best, it will be in the form of complaining; at worst, it will be by walking out the door. Decide for yourself which approach is best for your own office culture and employee morale. At the very minimum, you should have them printed for all of your staff to have posted by their workstations.

Once you've finalized your service standards, along with your vision, mission, and values statements, you will have completed a solid working foundation for your law firm—one capable of supporting exponential growth. You'll also have created a pretty amazing message.

5. What Is Your USP?

So many people struggle with identifying what their unique selling proposition (USP) is. One of the things that I say about the unique selling proposition is that it is not as complicated as you may think it is. Generally speaking, your unique selling proposition is very apparent to other people. Asking some of your clients why they hired you and why they were satisfied with the service you provided is one place where you can start identifying what your unique selling proposition is.

When I started 8 Figure Firm Consulting, one of my unique selling propositions was that I was a law firm owner who had actually reached eight figures in predictable revenue. This gave me the credibility to talk about what it was like to reach that level. I had been there, done that. I used this in my message a lot. I would spend time telling people I was a consultant, not a coach. A coach is someone who helps you get to the decision. As a consultant I was going to tell you what you were supposed to be doing. This was a big differentiator. Another part of the USP was that my focus was on implementation. This meant that I wanted to help you get things done. I wanted to make sure that you walked away with things to do and not just things to think about.

In the process of building my consulting business, I knew that I needed to use this unique selling proposition in every conversation. This, along with my vision, mission, values, and service standards, informed my clients and my staff of the full message I was trying to communicate to the world. And so, when I did a sales call, I always figured out a way to intertwine my vision and my mission, as well as my unique selling proposition, every single time.

What has come from this is that most of the people who hire 8 Figure Firm do so specifically because of the very unique selling proposition that I offer in my marketing materials. Sure, there may be other consultants out there who have a similar pitch. I am still not competing with them because they may have a different brand appeal. If I wanted to be like other consulting businesses, I could take myself out of the equation and stop promoting it as an attorney lead consulting business. But because I enjoy doing the consulting and the teaching, I've decided to stay with it until I find myself unable to scale. As of today, 58 law firms rely on 8 Figure for growth, and I haven't found it to be a detriment to market in this fashion.

You must find a similar way to distinguish yourself and then communicate the difference.

Regardless of whether you practice in an area of law that seems as if there is no clear way to identify yourself in a unique manner, the fact of the matter is that is not true. Every single business can distinguish itself because not every single business sells the same product. McDonald's and Wendy's both sell a hamburger. But the hamburgers they sell are dramatically different from each other. It is easy to see this in the context of burgers because they are products. But one thing you must keep in mind is that your law service is also a product. Once you begin to see it that way, you will figure out what packaging it needs and what message should be written on the box to ensure that the maximum number of people see it.

At the very core of the unique selling proposition is something that nobody can take away from you: your name. Your very identity is a unique selling proposition. The way you look is a unique selling proposition. The way you carry yourself is a unique selling proposition. The way you speak is a unique selling proposition. I don't want to go into too much of the brand appeal chapter here, but at the end of the day who you are and how you present yourself is a unique selling proposition even if no other proposition exists.

The personal injury space in Atlanta is saturated with lawyers. Yet, we have found that being two young lawyers who are aggressively building their law firm has been appealing to many people. Many of our clients have enjoyed the fact that we are two relatively young law firm owners who are building a successful practice and therefore "must know how to practice the law." You and I both know that this is not necessarily the case. But the client who is being repositioned with branding and being educated by our marketing does not have the same perspective as a well-trained lawyer who understands the industry.

How to Develop Your USP

Identifying your unique selling proposition can be a game-changer for you and your law firm. In the past, I've worked with some law firms that have very unique selling propositions simply by the nature of their niche and the fact that there's not a lot of competition in their practice area. And when you work in a practice area where there is an opportunity to niche down, it's important that you niche down with your unique selling proposition in mind. If you work in a practice area that is very saturated or there are many people who do something similar to what you do, you will have to be more intentional about developing and communicating your unique selling proposition.

The three steps I recommend to identify your USP are the following:

1. **Know your ideal client.** I am amazed at how many times I ask a law firm owner who their ideal client is and they say, "EVERYONE!" The fact of the matter is that not everyone is your ideal client. For me, my ideal client is a law firm owner between 35 and 55 years of age who has been stuck at the same revenue level for at least two years and currently does revenues of at least $1 million. I know that many of my clients do not fit this mold. But if I have to think of an ideal client, this would be the one.

2. **Identify what problems they have.** Once you know who your ideal client is, you want to write a list of problems they may have. Many of my clients have confidence issues, planning issues, and implementation issues. These are the reasons their law firms are not growing as fast as they want.

3. **Demonstrate how you solve the problem.** I solve problems by providing mindset coaching, having a specific plan for marketing that my law firm has used before, and having a program that provides implementation support.

All of this, combined with the fact that I was a law firm owner, created a very unique selling proposition for my business. Not only that, now I know what I need to communicate in my marketing to make it effective and efficient.

6. What Are Your Goals?

The last essential for your message is your goals. Yes, your goals. I know this may sound completely irrelevant, but it's not. Your goals will inform your audience of what you are trying to achieve. This year my goal is to have 100 lawyers signed onto our programs. This becomes part of the marketing message for people on the outside and for your clients.

Before you open a spreadsheet and begin totaling your expenses, take a step back. Without a clear objective, you'll get lost in the weeds, and as the saying goes, "failing to plan is planning to fail." When you set goals, you're also setting the destination. Without a destination, you can't chart your course.

If you're reading this book, it's probably safe to assume you've defined your goal as exponential law firm growth. When you take a hard look at it, though, it's kind of vague. To clarify this goal, work to understand what this objective looks like, in concrete terms, over the next 12 months, five years, and even 10 years. Of course, plans can and will change, and it's important to stay flexible, but spelling out your growth expectations in terms of actual numbers is important.

In addition to the profit and revenue numbers you'd like to see, it's helpful to visualize what these numbers mean to you in terms of your professional and personal life. *Why* do you want law firm growth? Do you want a better work/life balance? Do you want to build the biggest firm in your region? Do you want a vacation home in Hawaii? The more specific your endgame goals are, the less likely you are to become distracted along the way.

Your goals will inform what you are trying to achieve in your law firm. What you are trying to achieve in your law firm will determine the message that you want to put out to your community. When I was building 8 Figure Firm I wanted people to know that my goal was to have 100 law firms hiring our business. I wanted people to know that I wanted 100 law firms experiencing eight figures in predictable revenue. And so, I used this to inform my message. Not only was it part of my vision and mission, but it was part of every conversation that I had with individual clients and with my employees.

Putting It All Together in a Message

You have heard the six essentials to developing a message. But how do you put it together? How do you turn these six essentials into a cohesive message that you can communicate to all your clients and use to create an efficient marketing plan? This is sometimes the trickier part of the equation. I want to explain it in this section so that you can better understand how this message is going to create incredible efficiency in your business.

Once you have developed your vision and mission, you'll have something you can use to craft your message. When we were crafting our vision and mission for the law firm, we came up with the idea of inspiring hope and empowering people. We believed that if we could inspire hope and empower people in the community, we would be serving the greater good for a lifetime. We believed that the vision and mission would create generational benefit to all who came in contact with us. And so, our message came directly from that vision and mission.

We spent a tremendous amount of time trying to craft the message that would go out on the radio, TV, billboards, and social media. And what we settled on was that we were going to empower the injured. We wanted to empower them to win the most money in their case. We wanted to empower them to maximize their physical recovery. We wanted to empower them to no longer feel like a victim. This became the message that we would communicate in all our marketing.

Once we crafted the vision for 8 Figure Firm and tied the mission, core values, and service standards together, we arrived at a place where adding the unique selling proposition would accelerate the efficiency of our marketing. Our message to our clients was the following:

1. You can do this

2. You were made for more

3. There is a formula that you can follow

4. The formula works for every practice area

5. Trust the process

When you look at the majority of our marketing you will see that these five points are generally found in our message. And it is this message that makes us unique. This message, coupled with our experience and what we have developed as a product, entices people to call us and ultimately hire us to help them grow their business. In the same manner, when you have developed the six essentials of your message, the message will penetrate the noise of the marketplace and will eventually create efficiency in your marketing, leading to a lower cost of acquisition and higher profitability.

Get Ready to Grow

In the coming chapters, I'll give you the tools you need to harness the power of marketing so you'll be able to grow your firm exponentially. The strategies I've learned through my own law firm's journey are a blend of the entrepreneurial spirit and an understanding of the nuts and bolts of marketing. In today's world of data analytics, social media, and traditional marketing channels, there is no shortage of tools available to you. That said, it can be difficult to wade through the information you need to make these tools work for you. That's why I wrote this book.

CHAPTER 3

THE MINDSET
OF MARKETER

*"To be successful you have to be out there, you
have to hit the ground running."*

Richard Branson

As the incomparable Richard Branson notes, success is for
those who are ready to "hit the ground running." I whole-
heartedly agree with his philosophy, but there's something I'd
like to add. When you hit the ground, you need to know how to
run and where you're going. Throughout this book, I will help
you understand why marketing is a crucial component of law
firm growth and explain how we were able to utilize critical and
cutting-edge marketing strategies in expanding our firm to a
$30,000,000 valuation. If the destination is the 8 Figure Firm, the
marketing process is "the running."

In terms of marketing, learning how to run doesn't just
mean how fast you go but also how best to cross the terrain.
Intuitive marketing is about hopping off the proverbial treadmill
and covering massive ground. In order to develop the right
strategy for your marketing, you have to have the marketing

mindset. As a business owner, your primary responsibility is top-line revenue. Understandably, this is a hard concept for many lawyers to grasp.

Most lawyers go to law school to be lawyers, not necessarily to own a law business. Even those who look forward to the day when they own their own law firm, they think about the law firm in the traditional sense where the firm grows through the addition of partners who all bring in their own case loads. In the traditional law firm, there are two to 10 partners who are individually responsible for bringing in their own book of business. That book of business will generate enough work for two to three additional associate attorneys. The combination of the efforts of all of the partners minus the overhead will lead to better profitability than what can be generated by a solo law firm owner. That is the traditional model.

The law firm owners' responsibility in top-line revenue means they must take full control of 100 percent of the lead generation of the business. Would it be nice if a lawyer or an employee in the firm generated independent business? Sure! But in this new paradigm, the law firm owner is tasked with developing 100 percent of the new business. This is the marketing mindset that you must have.

The marketing mindset can prove elusive at first. I'm a prime example of how someone can be chest-deep in marketing tools and still not "get" it. What I didn't understand was that the true mindset of marketing requires more than hiring the best consultants and reading the most popular marketing books. While those tools can be beneficial, they won't be the reason you outpace the pack. If the mere act of attending webinars and listening to podcasts worked, almost every law firm would be an 8 Figure Firm. The turbo boost you need is the *mindset*.

So, what is this mysterious marketing mindset? Marketing is a race for insights that determines downstream success. The mindset is how you experience the journey. In the pages ahead, I will discuss the insights I learned on my path, and I'll explain where I went off course so you can avoid the same pitfalls.

Let me say this before you dive into this chapter headfirst. The marketing mindset requires you to believe in the predictability of human behavior, believe that you have a certain brand appeal, believe that there is an infinite amount of business for you to obtain, and believe that there is no greater investment in your life than the investment in your business.

You must treat your business as a stock. And the goal of the stock is to see the valuation of the business continue to rise each and every year. This mindset will completely change the way you invest in this stock.

The marketing mindset requires you to believe in the predictability of human behavior.

Moving Forward to Get Ahead

Inertia is a tricky beast. By definition, it is "a tendency to do nothing or to remain unchanged." Inertia is a common culprit behind a law firm's lack of significant growth. Although you might believe an 8 Figure Firm is on the horizon, and you hope your current practices will get you there, the hard truth is that if your current practices were going to get you there, you would be there.

Waiting for insights to come your way and hoping your business (or your luck) will improve ultimately leads to procrastination. It's easy to make excuses for your lack of growth when you aren't proactively seeking to change your marketing mindset. To get ahead, you'll need to get off the treadmill and take ground-covering steps toward that 8 Figure Firm on the horizon. You can do it, but you need to be prepared to own the truth. The truth is, if your current strategies were sufficient, you'd already be where you want to be.

The first step in the marketing mindset is that the marketer is always looking to create momentum. Momentum is the most important part of your marketing strategy. It is attained when you combine the right message with the right campaigns, using the right channels to reach your target audience.

Every week I hear another client tell me that they are not executing their marketing plan because they have more leads than they can handle, and they need to get operations right. This is absolutely not the right solution. If you want a fast-growing organization, you have to create momentum. If you are having problems with operations, you need to fix that. But never, ever stop creating momentum in your business just because you don't have the right people to handle it.

In 2020, our law firm was hit with the same pandemic that every other firm experienced. For whatever reason, we believed that if we just cut back on momentum in a couple of places, we would save some money, and when the pandemic was over, we would restart and everything would go back to normal.

In March of 2020 we started contacting our vendors and letting them know we would be placing holds on a lot of our marketing strategies, including several of our direct response channels. The pandemic shutdown did not last long in Georgia, and on April 29, 2020, everything was essentially back open.

However, we did not restart our marketing campaigns. We were still signing a significant number of cases at the time, and we were resolving way less than we were bringing in even though we had seen a drop in signups of almost 50 percent.

It took us almost nine months to finally pull the trigger and reengage some of the marketing we had stopped. By this time, it was January of 2021, and we were convinced we would jump back into shape. It didn't happen. As much as I hate to admit it, we did not get back into pre-pandemic shape for another whole year. Don't get me wrong, we were still bringing in more cases than we were resolving. However, we were 200 new clients per month short of our pre-pandemic levels. When we looked back and conservatively calculated how many clients we failed to convert because we stopped marketing, it was probably in the $15 to $20 million range. That is what we call a high-level mistake.

I tell you this as a cautionary tale so that you do not repeat the same mistake, which was stopping the momentum of lead generation. Do not stop marketing NO MATTER WHAT! It doesn't matter if you have the people. If you bring in the cases, you will find a solution.

The other day I was talking to a guy about the fight or flight response to situations. I told him that you cannot manufacture that response because it is a natural response to fear. When you get yourself into a situation where you fear you don't have enough people to handle your caseload, your fight or flight instincts will kick in.

Learning to Love the Journey

Once you've stepped off the treadmill and taken the first few steps toward developing an intuitive marketing mindset, you will discover that it can be a bumpy road. When I began my journey, I expected a somewhat smooth racetrack; instead, I was on a cross-country course. Rather than comfortable turf, I found I was traversing peaks and valleys and maneuvering around obstacles along the way. It's easy to get discouraged, but the key to success is learning to love the journey. Each valley is a learning experience that makes you stronger and better conditioned for the next. Each peak brings spectacular views and insights. Each obstacle adds to the experience.

In the marketing world, these roadblocks or setbacks may look like disappointing marketing campaign results or a poorly allocated budget. I *promise* you that even in those frustrations, you can find small wins. If you live or die by only good reviews, positive growth, and achieving big goals, you'll risk burnout. It's the journey along the way, and the celebration of small steps, that provides the fuel for the race. If you want to reach that 8 Figure Firm in your vision, you need to not just appreciate the journey but love it. When the journey becomes your passion, and not just a means to an end, you'll be unstoppable.

False Beliefs in The Marketing Machine

As promised above, you'll experience roadblocks on your path to marketing success. I've designed this book to provide you with a marketing roadmap to help you navigate through and around common false beliefs that can throw your journey off course before you even hit the ground. There's no shortage of rumored shortcuts to explosive growth, and while I'll be the first to say you should work smarter and not harder, that doesn't mean there's one universally reliable shortcut to an 8 Figure Firm. Here are five common pitfalls to avoid in your marketing journey:

False Belief No. 1: You just need one big win.

I know too many law firm owners who believe that their big win is just around the corner. The thinking is that they only need one bulletproof client, or one big case, to bring their firm the notoriety and revenue they deserve. The result of this approach is a lot of hoping and procrastination. You'll lose months or years waiting for the golden ticket when you could have spent that time excavating the gold mine itself by creating your brand in the marketplace.

Relying on luck as your roadmap to success ensures you'll miss the power of the small things that would otherwise bolster your business processes. Why chance it when you don't need luck in the first place? You need endurance and determination to build a wildly successful law firm—and these, to be honest, are easier to come by than luck anyway. You can and should build an 8 Figure Firm based on sound business practices—not chance.

False Belief No. 2: You will change.

Most law firm owners have a vision of what their firms will look like in the future. I know I did—in my vision, my future firm was profoundly successful, and I had time for my family. Ultimately, I was able to realize this vision, but it wasn't because I changed at my core. Most people don't fundamentally change. If your most productive hours are after 10 p.m., it's unlikely you're suddenly going to become a morning person. If you tend to procrastinate towards the end of the day, you probably won't start checking off everything on your to-do list after 4 p.m.

The good news is that you don't have to change. The key to success is figuring out how to leverage performance around your worst self. This approach may sound like I'm asking you to give up any and all self-improvement efforts, but I'm not. What I'm suggesting is that you identify those core traits that are unlikely to change and build in fail-safes. Restructure your day so you're handling the hard stuff during your peak hours of productivity, and putting off the important calls until after you've had your second cup of coffee and some breakfast. It's the little things that make the big picture work.

False Belief No. 3: More resources equal more success.

There are plenty of law firm owners or would-be law firm owners out there who think, "If I just had a little more capital, I could really get my firm off the ground." I'm here to tell you that this is a toxic marketing mindset that leads to inaction. Believing that it's not time to pursue growth because you haven't generated enough income to invest in marketing will cause you to run in circles. If your mindset is that you don't have enough resources because you can't grow your firm, and you can't grow your firm because you don't have enough resources, you'll be forever stuck in a negative feedback loop. At some point, you have to take the plunge and start spending money on marketing so you can generate a return.

The key to interrupting this vicious cycle of inaction is to focus on what you *do have* and make that your biggest strength until you can ramp up in those other areas. The truth is, you will always be constrained in some way, and the sooner you learn to think outside of your limitations creatively, the sooner your marketing mindset will become your superpower.

False Belief No. 4: You can buy your way into a marketing solution.

While some law firm owners believe they don't have enough resources, others believe resources will solve all of their marketing problems. The false belief that you can buy your way into a marketing solution that will win the search-engine war misses the point. If search engine optimization was never the problem, you'll have wasted time and money fixing something that wasn't broken—and you may have neglected or overlooked the real issues in doing so.

If you want your marketing machine to run like a Ferrari, you need to know how to maximize performance. You need to put the right investments into the right channels for the right amount of time. You don't polish the fenders when what you really need is an oil change. Developing a marketing mindset means learning where to put your resources to obtain peak performance. Tactics that work for some may be less helpful to others, and running an authentic marketing campaign that's true to your needs requires nuance and understanding more than anything else.

False Belief No. 5: You need to strengthen your weaknesses.

Of all the discussions I have with law firm owners looking to grow their firms exponentially, this is the false belief that's often hardest to eliminate. From a young age, we're all taught to strengthen our weaknesses, and if you're like me, you assumed this applied to marketing as well. I spent more than two years trying to strengthen my weaknesses, but our firm didn't explode with new clients until we began to strengthen our strengths. This concept is counterintuitive at first, but when you put it into practice, you'll find you're working more efficiently and effectively.

I believe that 80 to 90 percent of your profit will come from three things you do exceptionally well. This is the case in both business and personal life. In my personal life, I know that if I listened to my wife, spent quality time with her and affirmed her as a wife, mother, and friend, more than 80 percent of the job would have been fulfilled in our marriage. This can be said about your business as well.

When I think about my business and what I bring to the table, it boils down to three things: 1. Thoughtfulness, 2. Operational support, and 3. Sales. If I focus on just those three things, I believe the business will explode in a major way. But I have to focus on those things and not on my weaknesses.

Strengthening your strengths involves knowing when to delegate or outsource a task and when to double down on your personal efforts. For example, if you're a content marketing genius, you should invest time and energy into learning the latest strategies to stay ahead of the curve. If you can't seem to find success in your content marketing, hire someone with a proven track record to handle it. If you're not in a position to outsource this task, then learn what you can, but don't spin your wheels. Trust that if you put your energies where you can show the most improvement, the other puzzle pieces will fall into place. The strengthen your strengths marketing mindset requires two key components. First, you need to understand your strengths, and second, you need to focus your efforts there.

Winning the Marketing Race

I'll be the first to admit that marketing can be a grind, and you have to market if you want to build an 8 Figure Firm. That said, I've come to truly love the process, and you can learn to love it too. When you learn to market with your authentic voice and are true to your core values, you'll find that marketing becomes an extension of who you are and what your firm represents.

Winning the marketing race means learning to love the race itself. Let's face it, as a law firm owner, you'll always be marketing in some capacity, and when you embrace the process of your wins and your failures, you'll become a pro at problem-solving in all areas that affect the growth of your firm. The marketing mindset allows for critical thinking on various fronts, and when it starts to click, you'll realize just how vast the horizon is. Don't lose sleep on the constrained, rigid view of how you *thought* marketing worked. Instead, stay optimistic, accept radical responsibility for what isn't working, and put your energy into the big vision of that 8 Figure Firm on your horizon.

The first step toward harnessing the power of marketing is developing the mindset you need to move through the journey. Dive into the research resources available online (including the 8 Figure Firm resources we provide) and cultivate genuine curiosity. It is more than charts and numbers—it's human psychology that informs how individuals move through life, looking for ways to improve them. Beware of the false beliefs that can lead you astray, and don't rely on luck to get you where you want to be. Remember to play to your strengths and outsource the tasks that are simply outside of your wheelhouse. Don't forget that you can do a lot with a little, and big marketing funds don't always equate to big profit. Get creative and think outside of the box—it's more fun that way anyhow. Finally, understand that it is a lot of hard work, but if you embrace the lessons you learn along the way, marketing becomes an invaluable journey. This is the true entrepreneurial thinking that will turn your law firm *practice* into a law firm *business*.

CHAPTER 4

DEFINING YOUR LAW FIRM BRAND

"If people believe they share values with a company, they will stay loyal to the brand."

Howard Schultz

Your brand is critical to your success as an individual and a law firm. The brand is what everyone else sees and believes about you, whether you are aware of it or not. Everyone has a brand appeal. There is no denying it. Some people like my brand and some people don't. There is a group of people that would hire you just because. Then there is another group of people that would never hire you just because. You want to spend the majority of your time creating a brand that attracts the majority of the people to whom you already appeal.

Defining your brand is critical to creating momentum in the marketplace. Your brand appeal is made up of many factors. The way you look and present yourself to the marketplace will dictate a lot about the client base that will hire you. You may think that's not right. And that is okay. But your thoughts will not change the facts.

A brand takes many shapes and forms, but is summed up nicely by author Seth Godin, who explains, "A brand is the set of expectations, memories, stories, and relationships that, taken together, account for a consumer's decision to choose one product or service over another." In a sense, your brand is the sum of everything your law firm is about. The nature of your legal work, your billing practices, your community involvement, and everything in between work together to tell a story about your law firm brand.

There are an overwhelming number of opinions concerning the how-to of branding. Law firms looking to build or reshape their brands can easily find themselves up to their eyeballs in vague suggestions that offer no clear directive. Part of the problem is that a brand is an abstract concept, and it can be difficult to pinpoint the steps a law firm should undertake to accomplish effective branding goals. This doesn't mean effective branding is available only to the esoteric, creative types, though. There is, in fact, a coherent strategy behind excellent branding.

Wildly successful law firms have great branding, which they accomplished with the same attention to detail they applied to other law firm growth strategies. In this chapter, I'll give you specific, actionable steps you can use to inform your creative process while building your law firm's brand. Building and elevating a law firm brand requires a certain set of tools and an understanding of your audience. These tools will ultimately help you build a standout brand that will be the cornerstone of your law firm's growth.

Why Do You Need Branding for Your Law Firm?

I find it so unfortunate that many coaching and consulting companies out there do not teach the power of branding to more law firms. In fact, there are some that completely reject the concept outright even when the facts and the data say otherwise. For me, branding is the process of creating maximum exposure and awareness for your product. Your product, of course, is the legal service you provide. Just because you cannot directly track branding efforts and just because you cannot track the effectiveness of your brand, this does not mean that branding does not work. Branding absolutely works at growing your law firm if you invest the time and effort in developing your brand and sharing it with the world.

Branding your firm is the single greatest tool you can use for lowering the cost of acquisition for clients. When people wait in line for hours to pay hundreds of dollars for Nike shoes, they do it because of the brand and not because Nike has created a direct response campaign for their new shoe launch. It is easy to see this in another product but not so much in your own. I can tell you from experience that regardless of your product, if you have the right branding campaigns, over time you will see the result you are looking for.

Branding is equivalent to farming. Direct response marketing is equivalent to hunting. The question you must answer for yourself is whether you want to hunt for the rest of your life or build a farm whose harvest yields an unlimited return for you and your family for years to come?

The answer seems obvious. You want to be a farmer. Farming is branding.

Below I will walk you through the steps for effective branding.

Step 1: Build a Standout Brand through Storytelling

I remember once being in the audience at a keynote speech in North Carolina. The speaker got on stage and started with this incredible story of how he wanted to be a basketball coach but soon realized that basketball at the high school level did not pay the bills. He talked about the importance of goal setting and how goal setting was instrumental to his success. The stories hooked me instantly. Even though that speech was delivered over 20 years ago, I still remember him talking about going to work at a bank in his rusted car. Stories are powerful.

Law firm clients have specific needs, and these are frequently tied to emotionally heightened scenarios. A potential client might need a criminal defense attorney, or maybe they've been seriously injured due to another's negligence. Even corporate clients have emotional ties to the legal work they need from a law firm. While corporate client needs may not hinge on personal safety and comfort, you can bet they care about deadlines, political climates, and protecting their professional standing within their industries. In convincing a potential client that your firm is a good fit for their needs, you'll want to tap into these emotions.

When you're able to evoke the appropriate emotions from your audience through well-crafted branding, you'll be sending them a message that says, "we know what you need and we're here to help you through this issue and beyond." The most effective way to evoke emotions through branding is by telling a story. You don't need to tell just *your* story, though. Effective branding tells a story that sets the client as a primary character. Centering the client in your story helps you achieve specificity by demonstrating to the client through brand messaging exactly how their relationship with your firm will benefit them.

Focus on Outcomes

All too often when law firms are selling their services, they are only selling what they do. I remember being at a conference a while back where the speaker mentioned that clients do not need a lawyer. They need resolution. That resonated with me. When a client comes to your firm, they do not really want to hire you because you are great, or your firm is great. They want to hire you because they believe that you will provide them a great outcome.

When your brand is developed with the outcome in mind, the client will understand it better. Louis Vuitton does not sell handbags, remember: they sell status. When you wear their bags or shoes or clothes, you feel elevated in your status, walking around knowing that you could afford the high-priced item.

I think about restaurants like Chik-Fil-A (CFA) here in Atlanta. They do not sell chicken sandwiches. They sell comfort and convenience. For those of you not familiar with this restaurant, it is a fast food restaurant that brings your food to the table, has diapers for your kids and 50 people working the drive through, and is known for getting 16-year-olds to say, "my pleasure." Going to CFA is always a pleasurable experience. All of this is part of their brand.

You have a brand whether you have defined it or not. Your brand may be the hardass. Your brand may be the pushover. Your brand may be the appeaser. Your brand may be that you are incompetent. When you fail to focus on your brand, you will allow your brand to be what others say it is. The narrative will be dictated by others, which is no way to establish a truly strong brand.

When I think about the brand I am working to create with 8 Figure, I want to create the outcome of success. Success looks like more time and more money. Success looks like more freedom. Success looks like more connections. Success looks like more life experiences. For you, success could mean more vacations, more concerts, being season ticket holders at your favorite sports venue, saving more for your kid's tuition, buying a boat, having a second home, or just being there for your parents in their old age and having time to to go your kid's soccer games. The 8 Figure brand is all about that. If you do not focus on developing your brand, you will not be able to see this outcome in your own law firm or in the lives of your clients.

Specificity matters, and achieving uniqueness can be a difficult hurdle to overcome when your law firm origin story sounds like most others. To troubleshoot this problem, emphasize qualities and values that make you, and each of your clients, unique individuals. Wildly successful branding sends a message to current and future clients about why your firm is special. I believe your firm is special no matter the practice area. There is something about your law firm that is above and beyond better than anyone else in the marketplace. Have you identified that uniqueness and positioned yourself so that your brand would be known?

As you're working to develop a narrative that differentiates your firm from others who represent the same market, ask these questions:

1. What does your firm value in attorneys and staff?

2. What makes your firm unique among market competitors?

3. Who is your target client? No, it's not everyone!

4. What emotional impact will your legal services have on your clients?

5. How do your legal services improve your clients' lives beyond their immediate needs?

6. What is the story your clients will tell about you when the case is done?

7. What is the story your employees will tell about working at your firm?

8. What is the feeling people get working with you and for you?

These eight questions will give you a starting point for developing your law firm's story and brand. Knowing your firm's identity and your ideal client's identity is a crucial first step. The best branding is clear, but your message will be anything but if you don't know who you are or who you are speaking to.

Another reason to hone in on the motivations of your target audience is so you can deliver your message effectively. You wouldn't, for example, go to a comedy club and perform Shakespeare. Similarly, you shouldn't use sophisticated legal jargon to communicate with a client injured in a car accident. Language, imagery, delivery format, and even the way you conduct yourself in public speak to your brand's context and aid in delivering your law firm's story.

In working with amazing law firms, I have heard incredible stories of resiliency. Those stories become the fabric of the brand that these law firm owners create for their businesses. Some people were abused at home and became advocates for people in immigration matters. One was almost killed in a car accident by a drunk driver and decided to become a personal injury lawyer. Another had received an inheritance from an unknown relative (so lucky, right?) and wanted to help other families leave legacies for their children's children.

Use your story to create a brand that connects with your target audience in a powerful way.

Step 2: Elevate Your Brand Above the Baseline Promise

If you're managing a moderately successful law firm, you're probably doing several things really well, not the least of which is providing quality work at a fair rate. Too many managing partners looking to exponentially grow their firms hinge their brand on the promise of effective and efficient legal solutions. They don't understand why this brand messaging doesn't ultimately propel their firm's growth into the stratosphere. Clients do not care about this.

The problem with relying only on the message of "good lawyering for a reasonable rate" is that this promise doesn't separate your firm from the pack. Every lawyer in the personal injury space promises you that they will get you the most money or that they have the best customer service. Almost every other moderately successful law firm offers its clients effective legal solutions at a fair market rate. Even bad law firms make you this promise. When you emphasize this as the bedrock of your firm's brand, you're taking two steps in the wrong direction:

1. You're telling clients your law firm is just as good as other law firms without telling them why your law firm is better than other law firms; and

2. You're wasting time and energy on a message that is the baseline expectation of would-be clients in the internet age.

If you only meet the baseline expectation in the development of your brand, you will not have very much success in convincing potential clients that your law firm is the better option. Unlike LV, CFA, and NIKE, you rarely see a line of people waiting to go into a Gap store or Kentucky Fried Chicken or Adidas. Not that the latter are not good brands, but rather they have not created the pull for people in a way that almost necessitates a response from the consumer. Having a brand promise that is elevated above the baseline will help you stand out from the pack.

To elevate your brand messaging beyond the threshold promise, you need to understand that the law firm marketing landscape has seen dramatic changes over the last five to 10 years. Pre-internet, firms of all sizes could rely on word-of-mouth advertising and consistent corporate clients to generate profit, but that marketing model has undergone relentless reshaping. I actually believe if you built momentum in your law firm between 1990 and 2010, you have absolutely no idea how hard it is to build a law firm today. Those years saw an incredible boom in the law firm advertising space. I remember that until around 2010 most law firms still did not have a website. Those that capitalized on radio and TV instantly separated themselves by the mere fact that they were creating massive awareness in the market. But those times have changed. No longer can you rely on the bully techniques to build a brand. Social media has truly evened the playing field. Easy access to Google and the accessibility of connection through your phone have made the market extremely competitive. Now, clients can research firms and read reviews, and the fact is that no would-be client will hire a firm whose online presence implies anything less than the baseline.

Over the last four years we have had a dozen lawyers leave our firm and start their own for one simple reason: the barrier to entry has been lowered to the floor. It is so easy to start a law firm today and get clients. Of course, I am not suggesting it is easy to grow from there or even sustain it. But to start, all you need is a computer and a phone, and you are off.

The bottom line is that clients already expect value and integrity. They want to know why you are different and why you should be trusted. In fact, value and integrity are prerequisites, and while you should absolutely reinforce that messaging, it won't be enough to elevate your brand significantly. Ultimately, clients will base their hiring decision on what sets you apart from other firms, not what makes you the same.

Step 3: Craft a Brand that Speaks to Your Target Audience

In this book, I write a lot about understanding your destination before moving forward with any marketing campaign. This methodology holds true while crafting your brand, and before you can fine-tune your law firm message, you need to understand your ideal client. The best way to attract the clients you want is to deeply understand your clients' needs and wants. It's a lot like fishing: if you plan to catch the prize bass, you've got to know what lure to use and, of course, when and where to cast your line.

In terms of branding, you need to consider what your ideal client needs and what they value. The nexus of need and value is the key intersection of brand success. Below are some examples of common client needs and values.

Example No. 1: The Corporate Client

The corporate client is often the type of client with deep pockets and ongoing legal needs. These clients are great. They're sophisticated and can be relied on for consistent, long-term work. This would describe my law firm. We have had the same few attorneys doing work for us for three or more years. And every month we get a bill and pay the bill. More than ever, though, political pressures require corporate clients to demonstrate an evolved approach to the matters of the day.

- **Need:** Corporate clients need consistent and reliable legal work done at a reasonable rate. We need accessibility. We need things done quickly, and we need the lawyers to react to a multitude of situations.

- **Values:** These days, corporate clients may value inclusivity, diversity, or sustainability, and they're likely to seek legal partners who demonstrate a commitment to these values.

Example No. 2: The Entrepreneur

The entrepreneur is a go-getter willing to take risks. These clients frequently hire lawyers who can help them form the shape of their business model or navigate red tape. Some entrepreneurs have strong financial backing, while others are still working toward their big payday.

- **Need:** Entrepreneurs need flexible and creative legal work done at a reasonable rate.

- **Values:** Entrepreneurs may value niche experience and original solutions to their unique legal problems.

Example No. 3: The Regular Individual

The regular individual can encapsulate several types of client. This is the business-to-consumer type client we generally think of when we think about law firms. They might be car accident victims, criminal defendants, or aging parents who need to create an estate plan. These individuals are different from the first two examples in that they're often less experienced with the law, and they're less likely to require your services on a revolving basis. Their needs and values can be more granular, but to some extent they have overarching commonalities.

- **Need:** Regular individuals need competent legal guidance at a reasonable rate. They need to trust you. They need to know you will get them a resolution. They need to have their anxiety reduced.

- **Values:** These clients value communication and explanation. They aren't as well-versed in legal matters, and they want to know their needs are receiving quality, individual attention. They value emotional reassurance.

You'll notice that the needs of these client types are similar. Good legal work for a good rate is a foundational requirement. However, you'll find that their values differ, and that's the hook you can hang your brand on.

Step 4: Bridge the Audience Gap

Who is your audience? If you answered, "clients and potential clients," you're partially correct. Your audience isn't just clients, though; your audience is everyone. Those looking to grow their firms need to understand how their brand messaging is received by their entire audience, not just those needing a lawyer. I read a book recently that made a statement which, even if it is not backed by statistical data, rings true to me. The statement was that 97 percent of people will need a lawyer. They just do not need one today.

If that is the case, you have to be certain that you have brand alignment in all of your communications so that some audience members receive one message while others receive another. The disconnect can lead to problems. This disconnect represents a gap. Think of this gap as a physical space where key content falls into the abyss, never to be seen again. Audience gaps waste time and money, and you may not even realize you've got one. When you have a gap in your audience, your brand is not penetrating that group of people. Therefore, your cost for acquiring the 97 percent of clients who do not need you today but will need you tomorrow will continue to rise.

To identify whether there is a brand messaging gap between your audiences, start by dividing your audience into the following two groups:

1.   The Internal Audience

2.   The External Audience

The internal audience includes every employee or representative of your law firm, while the external audience is everyone else. It's important to understand these two audience distinctions because, too often, the internal brand messaging and the external brand messaging don't entirely comport.

You might be wondering why you need to worry about how your firm's employees and associates receive your brand messaging. After all, isn't the brand's purpose to attract and retain clients? Yes, your brand should attract and retain clients, but you can't expect to convey your brand effectively if everyone hears a different message. Imagine the game of telephone you played when you were a kid. Do you remember how corrupted the message was by the time it made its way down the line to the last person? This happens all the time to law firms who don't ensure their internal audience has a deep understanding of their brand's intent.

To illustrate this point, consider a law firm that wants to market itself as a one-stop-shop for all conceivable legal needs. This brand concept may seem like a great idea in today's instant gratification and client convenience era, but would the law firm's brand message translate? Here's how it's likely to play out:

- **Internal Audience Perception**: "We prioritize working fast and keeping costs low."

- **External Audience Perception**: "They never call me or take the time to explain anything."

In this example, the internal audience may feel they're offering clients convenience, but the would-be clients often receive a different message. It's important to bridge that gap so your brand doesn't lose its intention when it leaves your door.

The implementation of surveys is the best way to assess whether there's a disconnect between your intended brand messaging and how the brand is perceived. These surveys can be formal or informal, and you can even hire a third party to administer the questions. The important thing is that you survey both the internal and the external audience to identify the disconnects in your brand messaging. Only then can you begin working to close that gap. The more you can bridge the gap, the more in control of your brand messaging you'll be.

Step 5: Re-Brand When Necessary

If your firm's growth has been stagnant, you may need to consider re-branding strategies. Re-branding isn't a decision to take lightly because the costs can really add up. The re-brand of our law firm cost in excess of $100,000. Even deciding to change the color of your website requires web design professionals and can easily extend to signage and stationery. These costs can amount to thousands of dollars, and while the changes may be necessary, you don't want to re-brand on a whim. An additional consideration in carefully strategizing a re-branding campaign boils down to ensuring that your new brand strategy is effective and, in fact, different. Ask yourself how it will be different and why that difference matters. You should be able to answer these questions in concrete terms. If you have allowed your brand to take on a life of its own and you are ready to be intentional in your branding efforts, you may benefit from a re-brand.

Of course, if you're reading this book, you may already suspect that re-branding is a necessary undertaking for your firm. Some reasons you may need to develop a re-branding strategy could include:

- You're consistently attracting the wrong type of client

- Your current brand doesn't set your firm apart from competitors

- You've significantly reorganized your law firm
- Your firm wants to reshape its core values to fit contemporary politics
- Your current brand materials are outdated
- You have eliminated a practice area or added some
- You have added a partner or two
- You have let a partner go
- You have realized your color scheme was not effective
- You want to enter into a new market

Your reason for re-branding could be any combination of the bulleted points above and more. The extent to which you'll need to rebrand will depend on how deep the change needs to go.

Before you begin your re-branding campaign, you'll want to conduct surveys among past, present, and future clients if possible. It's important to understand the external perception of your firm before you make any significant changes so you can make the right changes.

Consider How Changes Will Impact the Big Picture

Remember, when you apply a brand change to one aspect of your firm's marketing materials, you will need to apply that change to all your marketing materials. In years past, this meant making sure your letterhead matched your business cards, but today's law firms must consider their online footprint in addition to those traditional marketing methods. The more consistently your brand is presented throughout the platforms you use for marketing, the more visible your materials will be on search engines like Google. Making sure your business internally brands correctly is also important. This will unify the brand with clients and employees.

Don't Feel Pressured to Make Every Change All at Once

When you identify the aspects of your brand that need modification, you might be tempted to knock out all changes in one go. You're a go-getter. Trust me; I get it! Take a moment, though, and consider the benefits of a more strategic re-branding rollout. If you want to augment several components of your branding, like your social media presence, your visual marketing materials, and your blog content, you should phase in these changes over a period of time that allows you to monitor metrics and evaluate effectiveness. Of course, you want to make sure you aren't developing inconsistent content over all of your platforms, but there is a benefit to making incremental changes so long as they are ultimately homogeneous. Even when we want to make all of the changes at once, we need to fight that urge and be prepared to just move the ball forward. Make a plan of implementation so that every week or every month you are adding a new element to the brand you have created.

Avoid Common Branding Mistakes

In wrapping up this chapter on branding, I want to go over some common branding mistakes. If some of the mistakes described below sound familiar to you, don't feel defeated. In fact, you should pat yourself on the back for taking steps to build your brand. Once you develop a more nuanced understanding of what effective branding looks like, you'll be able to course-correct. After all, the point of reading this book is to learn a better way of marketing.

Skimping on Your Branding Budget

Your branding budget should be about 60 percent of your entire marketing budget. That may seem like a huge chunk, but your brand is the most important component of your firm's identity. Clients want to know who you are and what you stand for before they make their hiring decisions, and your brand will be what ultimately sells them on your firm. As your budget grows more and more, you will see the cost of acquisition sink. You will want to continue to stack branding opportunities to maximize your brand. This may mean that eventually your branding overtakes the 60 percent rule and you are spending 70 or maybe even 80 percent.

Brand Inconsistency

Inconsistent brand representation is a big mistake many law firms make. A lack of consistent branding sends multiple messages to current and future clients. Another pitfall of inconsistent branding might be that would-be clients fail to recognize your firm as the most appropriate choice for their legal solution.

Think about it this way, do you eat at restaurants that don't consistently deliver on the promise of good food? If your favorite pizza joint is only serving up edible pepperoni 75 percent of the time, you're going to start going somewhere that's more reliable because the messaging you receive is "we can't get it right all the time, and that's okay with us."

Inferior Content

A huge component of brand building consists of marketing and putting content out there in the hopes of creating as many connections as possible. You can create content through blogs, emails, text, and video. Each one has a different efficacy rate but all of them should be employed as part of your branding strategy. Some firms choose to do their own content while others outsource. My recommendation is that you outsource things you cannot do and/or manage effectively. If you cannot do the content yourself and you are not good at managing a team of content creators, you should outsource. If, however, you believe you can do the work and/or you believe you can manage a marketing team, by all means bring it in-house.

Each method has pros and cons, but the final product is often lackluster, either due to errors or inconsistencies. As the saying goes, "the way you do one thing is the way you do everything." Inferior marketing content sends a message to current and future clients that your legal work may be similarly plagued with errors or inconsistencies.

Remember, the client does not want a lawyer, they want a resolution.

You can boost the quality of your content in several ways. First and foremost, ensure your content focuses on the specific needs of your clients. Second, ensure your content is free of errors. Finally, deliver content regularly. The last point probably the most important of all. You should be posting content nonstop every single day. There are only a handful of social media platforms where the majority of law firm clients go. You should be posting there daily. You should also be delivering no fewer than two emails per week to your client base. Yes, some people will get annoyed, but they can just unsubscribe from your mailing list. Those who stay will be constantly reminded of you. Lastly, you should be posting blogs, articles, and videos online through your website and through YouTube.

When you apply these basic rules, your audience will extrapolate a positive message about your firm that extends far beyond the content itself.

Centering Yourself Instead of Your Client

Although your brand is your story, it is a mistake to center it entirely on yourself. In blogs, articles, and other forms of content, talk less about how you've built your firm and more about how you can help the client. There is a time and a place to provide your origin story, and your client should be able to access that when they choose. The "About Me" page on your firm's website is an excellent location for those details.

The brand needs to be about the outcome you will provide for the client. Spend time thinking about that outcome. What is it that the client will get when they work with you? How will the service impact their life long-term? How will your law firm help their family? What is the promise that you are delivering to the client? Remember, the client does not want a lawyer, they want a resolution.

Your Brand Isn't Distinct

In crafting your brand, it can be a great idea to take inspiration from other firms performing well in your market. That said, you'll want to avoid mirroring their branding too closely. Color schemes, font, website design, and even advertising templates can cause issues if they are too indistinguishable from your competitors'. Whether consciously or subconsciously, firms developing their brands often fail to create a vision distinct from other firms.

If your brand is not distinct, the brand with the most money will win the day because they will have more power in the market to spend on getting their name out. Make sure that your brand is unique, tell the story, create the content, and do it consistently over an extended period of time. This is the recipe to creating predictability in the marketplace.

CHAPTER 5

CLARIFYING THE CUSTOMER JOURNEY

"Get closer than ever to your customers. So close that you tell them what they need well before they realize it themselves."

Steve Jobs

Your clients are on a journey. The best way to make sure that journey is a positive one is to script it out and be intentional about taking them along for the ride.

According to Tiffany Hsu and Sapna Maheshwari of the *New York Times*, "People don't simply buy things anymore. Like epic heroes, they go on a customer journey that begins when they become aware of a certain product, continues through the time when they weigh whether or not they would like to have it, and reaches a conclusion when they buy it."

That is all to say, the term "customer journey" is used in the marketing sphere to describe the points of interaction that a potential client, aka "lead," will have with a brand, from their first contact through to their first purchase. But I want to take it a step further to say that the journey is even longer than that.

It should extend beyond the point of sale until the client no longer wants the relationship. This could mean a lifetime of contact and interaction points.

These interaction points are also known within the marketing sphere as "touchpoints." Touchpoints include marketing emails, social media posts, website visits, text messages, video delivery, and any other interaction a lead has with your brand. As potential customers evaluate a company, they will double back to touchpoints they've already visited, resulting in a customer journey that is anything but a linear path moving directly from Point A to Point B. The closer your touchpoints bring you to your customer during their journey, the more convinced they will be that they need to hire your firm.

The customer journey can prove confounding when you're trying to anticipate which touchpoints will be most effective. Understanding the process, though, is paramount to marketing success. Ultimately, there are proven steps you can take to clarify the customer journey and what it means both for you and your potential clients.

While there can be an overwhelming amount of nuance in analyzing the customer journey, I've learned that it all boils down to a handful of concepts. To bring your customer journey into focus, you need to:

- Define your objective.
- Identify and segment customer personas, then hone the stages of the journey for each customer segment.
- Determine the when, where, and how of your touchpoints.
- Put the customer journey map into action and collect data and feedback to analyze and improve friction points and constraints.

In this chapter, I've broken out the bulleted points above into actionable steps that anyone can implement in clarifying their customer journey and marketing goals overall.

I believe the customer journey is one of the most important pieces of your marketing. After you have your message and your brand, the customer journey will help develop the depth you need in your marketing for predictable referrals for a lifetime.

Step 1: Defining the Objective

At the start of any journey, especially the customer journey, it's important to know the objective, not only for your customer but also for you. In the legal sphere, potential clients are ultimately looking for solutions to specific legal problems. Too many law firms market themselves as a jack-of-all-trades when they are, in fact, deeply rooted in a specific niche. If the attorneys at your firm have tons of experience representing plaintiffs in medical injury cases, then you don't want to oversell the DUI defendant you represented that one time. It can prove counterintuitive—why wouldn't you think that diversifying your firm's practice means you'll get more clients? While different practice groups within a firm should certainly market to their strengths, your potential customer needs to be convinced that you are an expert in your field and that that is why they need your services.

You might worry that your law firm's niche isn't conducive to repeat clients—for example, if you offer services relating to mass torts or wrongful death claims. These clients still offer referral possibilities, though. If you aren't looking at the entire journey from the very start, it will be more difficult to get the most out of every aspect of marketing.

If, at first, you're unsure of how to define the objective for your customer, consider revisiting your brand messaging. If your brand isn't crystal clear to you, it will be difficult to convince an external audience of anything concrete. The customer needs to know why they should hire your firm, and your brand should be able to do significant legwork in convincing them.

Branding is a critical component in setting the tone for the customer journey from the outset. Law firms with excellent branding accomplish at least two separate goals. First, the firm that's undertaken the task of developing and elevating its brand will have a strong understanding of who *they* are. These firms have not only defined their objective; they're also executing it. This brings me to the second point: a firm that lives and breathes its brand conveys a clear objective to its current and future clients. A strong sense of brand identity prevents the issue of sending mixed signals to your internal and external audience.

The objective of the customer journey is fourfold:

1. **Establish connection.** Just because you know someone does not mean that you are connected to them. Your customer journey should create connection points between you and unknown people. How does this happen? It reminds me of something my old mentor used to tell me all the time, "I like your friends because I like you." The customer journey creates likability with your clients and therefore establishes a direct, or some may argue, an indirect connection between you and the unknown potential client.

2. If you have a customer journey where the client gets a gift upon hiring, then a reassurance video, then a welcome email, then a phone call from a legal assistant, and then a phone call from the attorney, and all of this happens within 72 hours, it is very likely that your client is going to like you more and communicate this with others when the time arises.

3.   Knowing that this is an objective will help you establish the touch points and the content that must be delivered at each point in the journey.

4.   **Build trust.** Trust is built in two different ways: earned or imputed. In either scenario, your customer journey can deliver on building more trust. As the client experiences your customer journey, they will begin to naturally trust you more. People tend to trust others when there is a genuine commitment to helping them succeed.

5.   If you want to test out this theory, go and offer any organization money for a scholarship. Or go and offer to pay for lunch for a group of unknown people. Will they trust you more or less? The answer is more. Even if they do not know you, they will trust you almost instantaneously. Your customer journey has this similar effect. When you are giving above and beyond the baseline expectation, the client will begin to develop an almost certain belief that you are genuinely there to help them. This trust will reduce terminations and increase referrals.

6.   **Reassure the decision.** When a client hires your firm, they are afraid, anxious, and stressed. There is nothing worse than adding a sense of buyer's remorse to those feelings. When you have a defined customer journey you can cut this buyer's remorse before it even takes hold by reassuring the client that they made the right decision. This could be done with a well-placed text message or a video. Regardless of how you deliver it, if you are intentional, you will more than likely be able to prevent any client from terminating your services or asking for a refund.

7. **Develop the relationship**. As you define the objectives of your journey, realize that people do business with people they know, like, and trust. Relationship building must be genuine and authentic. When done correctly, you will establish a relationship that lasts a lifetime. I have a client that my firm represented back in 2008. Fifteen years later, that client continues to send me referrals. Your journey should develop and build upon the relationship you have now established.

Step 2: Identifying Customer Personas

You cannot clarify the customer journey if you don't clarify who your customer is. Identifying customer personas is the key to understanding how best to target potential clients through marketing campaigns. First and foremost, you should accept the fact that not every customer is meant to be yours. This thinking can be a difficult hurdle to overcome for that competitive litigator in all of us, but consider this: when you're fishing for bass, you don't want to catch minnows. The same is true for law firm clients.

To consistently and reliably land the ideal client time and time again, you need to know everything about that client. Where do they live? What do they want and need? What attracts them? When you know the answer to these questions, you can target your messaging. Start by building out a fictitious customer persona that will enable you to see exactly where you can collect stats to inform your best marketing practices.

To build your customer persona, you need to be able to answer the following questions. You should get as much specificity as possible.

- What is their personal demographic and socioeconomic background?

- What do they eat?

- Where can you find them?

- What is their education level?

- Where do they work, and what is their position in their job?

- What do they do for fun?

- Where are they getting their information?

- What information do they consume?

I understand that, at first, these questions might seem out of place when you're trying to secure clients who, for example, need a criminal defense lawyer. You should ask yourself, though, would you rather defend the doctor in a DUI case or the 20-something kid with nothing to lose and spotty income? This is why customer personas matter and why you need to identify them to get the most out of your marketing campaign.

Identifying customer personas is the key to understanding how best to target potential clients through marketing campaigns.

You can have multiple customer personas so long as your message and brand are aligned in the way you communicate to them, even if the copy of what you are communicating is different.

Step 3: Segmenting Customer Personas

Segmenting customer personas means developing more than one customer persona. If your firm has multiple practice groups, you probably don't need to be told there is value in creating multiple customer personas. What may be less obvious, though, is that there is also tremendous benefit in identifying multiple customer personas even within the same legal niche.

Consider an estate planning law firm whose bread and butter is preparing wills and trusts. It's apparent that you'd want to develop a customer persona that fits the mold of older individuals seriously considering their posthumous wealth distribution. It's important to consider, though, that the children and relatives of those older individuals may initiate the estate planning process. Accordingly, it's worthwhile to build out their customer personas as well. It also shouldn't go without saying that younger people often understand the value of estate planning and will want to get their own affairs in order. Within this example legal niche, there are already three separate customer personas—the older client, the relative of the older client, and the younger client.

In addition to segmenting customer personas based on *who* will be seeking your services, it's vital to segment based on *how* individuals will be seeking your services. Utilizing the example above, older prospective clients are less likely to see your advertising on social media than they are in print. To split hairs even further, a wealthy young entrepreneur is apt to use their smartphone while someone in their 50s is more likely to use a desktop computer. Knowing who you are trying to reach will help you create the right marketing campaigns.

Step 4: Figuring Out Each Stage of the Customer Journey for Each Segment

Once you've defined the objective, identified your customer personas, and segmented them, it's time to refine the journey for each customer. The customer journey encompasses key stages that take your leads from brand awareness, through deliberation, and to the acquisition of your services. Many mistakenly believe that the customer journey stops once a client signs the retainer agreement when, in fact, the journey continues.

When you land a new client, you can go ahead and pat yourself on the back, but your marketing efforts can't stop there. Client retention is the next key stage in the customer journey, followed by advocacy. When clients reach the advocacy stage, their loyalty to you and your firm generates new leads through word-of-mouth referrals (more on referrals later).

So, what does it look like for a high net-worth client to move through the customer journey? Let's examine how the ideal lead may navigate the customer journey in their search for an estate planning attorney.

- *Awareness*—A doctor nearing retirement needs estate planning legal services, and she comes across your advertisement in a medical publication she subscribes to. She decides she needs to go ahead and get the ball rolling, so she investigates further.

- *Deliberation*—The doctor visits your website and checks out your bio page and blog. The blog informs her of numerous missteps people make when they don't seek out competent legal help. She decides to fill out the contact form and submits a general inquiry.

- *Acquisition*—You make a timely response to the doctor and schedule a meeting. She comes in, likes what she sees and hears, and hires your firm to set up a living trust.

- *Retention*—A year later, the doctor needs to amend her living trust to account for a beneficiary's untimely death. She reaches out to you again because you professionally handled her needs the first time around and perhaps also because the firm holiday card you sent to all of your clients is still on her fridge. And oh, by the way, she also needs assistance with the beneficiary's probate.

- *Advocacy*—Every encounter the doctor has had with your firm has made her life easier. As it turns out, she has a lot of demographically similar colleagues and friends who would benefit from your legal services too. When they mention to her that they really need to get their estate planning in order, she says, "You should call *my* lawyer."

Each customer persona will experience the customer journey stages differently, which is why you need to develop and segment the personas before you fine-tune how you want to present each stage to them. Leads will often circle back from one stage to another during the journey, and you can't let up on the gas once they've decided to onboard with your firm. The Retention and Advocacy stages of the customer journey are your return on investment, and you should work hard to secure that benefit.

Step 5: Determining When, Where, and How Touchpoints Work Effectively

Touchpoints are interaction points between your law firm and your clients or potential clients. Each time an individual experiences a touchpoint with your brand, they get to know you a little better. If you're doing your marketing job well, the seeds of loyalty begin to germinate. While touchpoints look different for each customer at each stage, that doesn't mean you can't successfully funnel and guide clients through to the next point on the customer journey with a fair amount of precision. When brainstorming touchpoints, it's effective to think about them in the Before, During, and After phases of their acquisition of your services.

Phase 1: Before the acquisition of your services

Before a lead becomes a client, they need to learn that you exist. This phase is where marketing pros do the heavy lifting. Touchpoints before hire look like paid advertisements, social media interactions, word-of-mouth referrals, testimonials, reviews, and exploration of your website and blog. Your presence in the community is also a significant way to maximize touchpoints; for example, you could offer an annual scholarship or participate in local volunteer efforts (we discuss more marketing methods later on in this book).

Phase 2: During the acquisition of your services

Phase 2 touchpoints come after the potential client has become a client, and while that doesn't mean they won't circle back to Phase 1 touchpoints, it does mean that you need a new touchpoint strategy specifically for them. Remember, the idea is to end the customer journey with as much return on investment in the Retention and Advocacy stages as possible. This means that you can't stop while you're ahead, and you'll need to leverage new touchpoints.

Phase 2 touchpoints are everything from how you and your staff personally interact with clients, to the way your office looks, to a holiday card. Customer service is the name of the Phase 2 touchpoint game. Communicate this to your staff, and don't forget that they play a critical role in business development.

Phase 3: After the acquisition of your services

Brainstorming Phase 3 touchpoints may be challenging at first. After all, you've already done great work for the client, and there's a possibility that they'll remain loyal even without the extra push. The best marketing strategists know that a "possibility" isn't good enough, and that should be your mindset, too, if you want to build an 8 Figure Firm. When you close a case for a client, you should ensure that follow-up touchpoints work in favor of client retention. For instance, if the client has billing questions, answer them promptly, effectively, and politely. To that end, if a third party handles your billing, do your own due diligence in ensuring they prioritize customer service.

Phase 3 touchpoints may also involve a request for a referral or a review of your legal services. While it may seem counterintuitive to ask something of a client, you can frame the ask in a way that shows you care about the client's feedback. The key here is giving the client everything they need to provide effective feedback without any inconvenience to them.

Step 6: Putting the Customer Journey Map into Action

At this point, you've collected and refined the tools you need to implement your customer journey map. You know what your objective is and who your customers are, and you know how your customers should funnel through each stage of their journey. Knowing how something is supposed to work is, however, no substitute for putting the plan into action.

First and foremost, consider implementing your firm's customer journey map through a group effort. Each member of your team, from the receptionist to the partners, will interact with clients, so they are also touchpoints. They need to know how the map dictates their role in the journey. Accordingly, you need to communicate your expectations to them. Everyone plays a part, and as they say, teamwork does, in fact, make the dream work.

When you communicate the plan to your dedicated team, it may help to provide visual tools. You can explain the process through charts and tangible markers. There is an assortment of templates online, and I've also included more discussion on mapping in this book.

Finally, begin rolling out each component of the customer journey map in phases. Not only can it be cumbersome to greenlight every step simultaneously, but it will be more difficult to track analytics.

Step 7: Collecting Data and Feedback

The customer journey cycle is ever-evolving, and one way to ensure you're on top of both natural changes and friction points in your planning is through the collection of data and feedback. You can DIY data collection through the use of Google Analytics reports and website hosting dashboards, and by directly asking your clients for their feedback. It can take some finesse to get helpful information from clients without also overreaching, but if you ask them what touchpoints were helpful to them and which ones may have even seemed to be in the way or were overkill. Be sure to frame your inquiries in a way that helps the client understand that you're making an effort to improve *their* experience.

Below are some useful ways to collect client feedback:

- Provide client surveys

- Give clients multiple opportunities to share feedback

- Use social media monitoring tools to see what clients say

You can also use third-party data analysts if your marketing budget allows. Whether you outsource data collection or prefer to be hands-on, you need to know what's working and what's not to fine-tune your marketing machine.

Step 8: Utilizing Data and Feedback

Mapping the customer journey serves dual purposes. Not only does it allow you to funnel your leads to your services, but it also provides an organized way to analyze which aspects of the customer journey are or aren't working.

You don't just want to focus on the problem areas, but, as I discussed earlier in this book, you should capitalize on those areas that come across strong. Ask yourself if you could improve upon your strengths.

Step 9: Analyzing Problems and Improve

Of course, you need to address the problem areas and troubleshoot so that you aren't squandering valuable time and resources on a strategy that isn't working for you. This step can be discouraging, but success is so often a numbers game, and it's those who are willing to keep trudging through who ultimately win the day. You will have failures—it's inevitable. It's how you navigate those failures that matters.

The customer journey should be in a constant state of refinement. When we first implemented the customer journey in our law firm it took nine months. One month later we made a change. Always be ready to pivot by adding into or taking something out of the journey that is not working. This will give you a greater chance at succeeding in creating true connection with clients that leads to more referrals.

Step 10: Repeat Steps 1 Through 10

The key to nailing down your customer journey is your willingness to refine the process through repetition. The value in tracking data during the various stages of the customer journey for each customer type is in the nuanced understanding such tracking gives you to tweak the process. Not only can you change what isn't working, but you can strengthen what *is* working. Certain aspects of the process may become less valuable over time, and unless you're working the steps, you won't know when to make changes.

Technology changes, industries change, and client preferences change. And those are only the predictable changes—if the COVID-19 pandemic has taught us anything, it's that things change, and to stay on top of the game, you need to evolve. Repetition of the steps ensures that your marketing strategies evolve with both the seen and unforeseen variables.

Realize that before you can market to your potential clients, you must understand who they are, where they are, and what they want. This knowing is achieved by working your way through each step of the customer journey through the eyes of your clients, keeping in mind that you have a variety of client types. Develop specific customer personas for each type of client, so you can direct your advertising to them. Understand why they need you before the ad ever reaches them. As you develop your knowledge of your customers' journey, track analytics and feedback to adjust course when the strategy isn't working. Work through the process frequently because your plan will inevitably need to evolve.

CHAPTER 6

DEVELOPING MARKETING CAMPAIGNS

"Concentrate your time, your brains, and your advertising money on your successes. Back your winners, and abandon your losers."

David Ogilvy

Lawyers are spending too much time trying to figure out what marketing channel to use instead of what marketing campaign will reach their target audience. What is a marketing channel? A marketing channel is a specific pathway for reaching your intended audience. You can think of a marketing channel as a means of delivery. It is the road that connects you to the client and the client's awareness of you.

You can deliver your brand and marketing materials through a variety of channels. While marketing channels have been around for 50 years, some of the most effective channels were ushered in with the internet age. Depending on your audience, you may need to focus on those tried-and-true marketing channels, or you may find more success through more contemporary means. At first, determining which channels work best for you can be difficult, but if you pay attention to the analytics, you can adjust course along the way. You'll increasingly learn how best to focus your marketing resources.

Locating the marketing channels that will work best for your firm is critical in experiencing huge growth. The process can initially seem daunting as the sheer number of options is overwhelming, but just as I discuss in other chapters of this book, all you need to do is get started. As you grow and learn, you'll be able to make informed adjustments along the way to an 8 Figure Firm.

But channel marketing alone, although necessary, will be inefficient if you do not understand the concept of marketing campaigns.

Marketing Channel vs. Marketing Campaign

Before we dive into the marketing channels available to you, I want to take a moment to distinguish marketing channels from marketing campaigns. These two concepts share similarities and are often used interchangeably by those new to marketing strategies. Without a campaign, you do not have a strategy for marketing. You can think of it like this: the marketing campaign is the umbrella under which you'll find the marketing channels. The campaign is the strategy, while the channel is the execution of that strategy. For example, you may launch a social media marketing campaign, but within that campaign, you'll utilize various channels, including Facebook, Twitter, or LinkedIn, to name a few.

Campaigns are developed by asking the question, "Where can I find my client?" The answer to the question will tell you where you should spend your marketing dollars.

Inbound Marketing Campaigns

The marketing campaign is where your strategy begins. Carefully planned campaigns are important, and they help motivate your team to meet goals within a certain timeline while staying within a budget. They are also critical in focusing your attention on the marketing materials you're really trying to implement. There are several clever campaign strategies that work well for law firms.

Often law firms find the most success with inbound marketing strategies, meaning marketing campaigns designed to attract potential clients. One reason this strategy is so widely used is that law firms are beholden to ethics rules that vary from state to state, which limits the use of other outbound marketing. Always, always, always make sure you're following your state's ethics rules and laws when implementing your marketing campaigns.

Inbound marketing campaigns will often focus on any of the following: content creation, SEO optimization, Google ads, pay-per-click, video creation, press releases, and referral network growth. Within these marketing campaigns, law firms can utilize several channels to execute their plan.

There are three primary types of campaigns with an endless combination of channels that you can use to achieve the end goal.

1. **Awareness campaign.** This is an impressions campaign and what we generally think about when we discuss branding. The objective of an awareness campaign is to get the greatest number of impressions in front of your target audience. The channels that you use for this type of campaign depends largely on where your clients can be found.

2. At 8 Figure Firm, I developed a hypothesis that my clients could be found on social media. I looked at the target age, demographics, and locations of the potential clients to inform this belief. The basis of this conclusion was also found in the countless amount of lawyer forums that existed on Facebook. When I

started to develop my awareness campaign, I wanted to zero in on the most effective platforms to put my advertising. I settled on Facebook, YouTube, and LinkedIn. Once I determined the channels I was going to use for this strategy, I needed to assign the spend. Spending would be based on the number of impressions I believed I could generate from each platform and my marketing budget.

3. **Perception campaign.** This is a reputational and messaging campaign. The purpose of this campaign is not only for people to know you, but also for potential clients to know about you. This is where you focus on delivering the message in a way that attracts people to want to know more. Unlike an awareness campaign where the goal is maximum exposure, the perception campaign seeks to build depth in the connection.

4. You may be thinking, "Why not do both in one campaign?" The answer may surprise you: you may not be able to. Think about it, it is very hard to build a message on a billboard when the potential client only has two seconds to read it. The purpose of the billboard is impressions. However, the perception of your company could be developed on your website where you write engaging content or record engaging videos for potential clients to know about you. The goal of a perception campaign is not to create awareness but rather to establish the perception you want people to have about your law firm.

5. **Sales campaign**. The purpose of this campaign is to sell. This is where you want to persuade people to purchase your product. The entire campaign is geared towards conversion. This strategy would implement

things like discount offerings and pay-per-click landing pages.

Ultimately you will want to use all three marketing campaign strategies and select the marketing channels that best achieve the objective of the campaign. If you start with the channels without giving thought to what you want to achieve, you will fail miserably, even if you sign up some clients.

Marketing Channels

There are a huge variety of marketing channels available to you. In fact, the sky's the limit, and as long as new methods of message delivery become available, new marketing channels will continue to abound. For example, email is now an indispensable marketing channel, but it wasn't a common marketing tool until the 1980s. Similarly, Facebook wasn't on anyone's radar in the early 2000s, but now most law firms have a Facebook page and Facebook marketing is a huge part of the strategy. Educating yourself about new marketing channels is important. Some marketing channels are so important, your absence from them will be a giant red flag to potential clients.

Some of the more common successful marketing channels used by law firms include email, blogs, social media, TV advertising, print advertising, billboard advertising, newsletters, radio advertising, and digital subscription advertising. These channels are great for inbound marketing campaigns as they allow you to deliver content that will attract an audience back to you.

Here is a little secret: almost any channel will work if the channel is where you find your client. What I mean by this is that if your target audience is 65 and older, it is not likely that you will find your client on Facebook. So, although Facebook would work, the cost of using Facebook for this demographic would result in a dramatically high cost of acquisition. That does not mean that Facebook doesn't work.

When I hear a client tell me that a marketing channel doesn't work, I instantaneously know they have not analyzed their target audience, determined where the audience could be found, and developed a campaign to reach them.

Because, remember, people are predictable. But if the people you want don't know about you, they can never hire you. You have to go where they are.

Using Marketing Campaigns to Focus on Your Marketing Channels

A marketing campaign should always be used when launching new marketing materials through various channels. The word "campaign" sounds very formal, and the plan certainly can be formal, but it doesn't have to be. If you're just starting out, consider how a plan will help you focus on the end goal while staying within a budget. Organizing the marketing endeavor as a campaign means you have a plan, and plans are crucial in both gaining and gauging success.

The Pros and Cons of Multi-Channel Marketing Campaigns

We've discussed marketing campaigns and marketing channels; at this point, these terms shouldn't sound too complicated. They don't have to be complicated at all, but big campaigns can sometimes call for multi-channel marketing initiatives that can quickly grow complex. When multi-channel marketing campaigns are launched across several platforms, the data analytics alone can be voluminous. Still, as your firm grows and your understanding of law firm marketing becomes more sophisticated (if it isn't already), you'll almost certainly undertake a multi-channel marketing campaign at some point. Let's discuss some key pros and cons of multi-channel marketing.

Pro: You Can Reach Thousands of People Instantaneously

One huge reason to implement a multi-channel marketing campaign is the volume of people you can reach. All too often, I see lawyers focused on just one channel, hoping that it never runs out of clients. Whether it is social media or traditional media, there is a limited supply of people that will like you and hire you, as you recall from the brand appeal chapter. Your goal is to go after the low-hanging fruit that automatically finds your brand appealing. You want to hit every channel where those individuals can be found.

If your campaign endeavors to draw in audience engagement through content generation, you can post links to numerous marketing channels, including LinkedIn, Facebook, and Twitter. You can also utilize SEO so your content is more visible on search engine results. If you're presenting new content in the form of a blog or a video, you only have to generate the content in one place, yet you can attract a massive audience to your website through a multitude of channels.

Having a multi-channel marketing campaign allows you to create a halo effect around your target audience.

Pro: Multi-Channel Marketing Can Be Easily Delegated

Multi-channel marketing can reach a big audience with less effort, especially if you're targeting online platforms. There are any number of professionals who can help you get the message across, and some law firms even find success by delegating content management and disbursement to a person or department in-house. While developing the content to be dispersed often requires more in-depth expertise, delivering the content through the channels can be delegated.

There are vendors that specialize in everything. You can have a TV media buyer, radio specialists, Instagram specialist, etc. Until you are ready to have an in-house marketing team, multi-channel marketing will allow you to have specialists in different areas of expertise aligning with your brand and message and creating synergy across multiple channels that hit your target audience. This is a powerful weapon in getting out your name and message.

Con: Ensuring Consistency Across All Channels Can Be Difficult

One of the biggest drawbacks to multi-channel marketing is the attention to consistency it requires. You cannot start a multi-channel marketing campaign until you have clarity of brand and message and have aligned your vendors to deliver this brand and message consistently in the channel that you are using. This can be one argument in favor of having a dedicated person or staff tasked with managing the rollout because inconsistency will send your clients mixed messages. It's not uncommon for your audience to participate in multiple channels, and if they receive different messages through different channels, they're likely to be turned off. Remember, inconsistency can communicate a bigger issue that reflects a law firm's overall attention to detail and work product.

Another reason inconsistency can be detrimental to your marketing campaign is how search engines raise or diminish visibility based on consistency. The more consistent you are throughout each platform you interact with, including pages within your own website, the more legitimate Google and other search engines will believe you to be. Inconsistency translates to banishment into online obscurity.

Con: Multi-Channel Marketing Can Be Expensive

The cost of multi-channel marketing can quickly add up to the tens of thousands. If you've planned and budgeted for these expenses, that's great, but if you haven't carefully considered the costs associated with the implementation and management of multi-channel marketing, you could find you're spending more revenue than you're generating. To manage your budget, start with just a few channels and carefully measure metrics that tell you what's working and what isn't. You can then add a few more channels and utilize those earlier metrics to help you refine your strategies with the additional channels.

The Best Marketing Channels for Your Firm

There are a few ways to approach choosing the best marketing channels for your firm. The savvy law firm marketing strategist will use a combination of methods to hone in on which channels they're likely to see the most return on investment from.

Research Competitor Law Firms

When building your campaign strategy and determining which marketing channels will prove most fruitful for you, you should look to other successful firms for inspiration. There's a bit of an art to researching the marketing methods of other law firms, and you want to make sure you're using your time wisely. Otherwise, you're apt to get lost in the weeds. It's more helpful to peruse their social media and take notes on what kind of recent content gets the most audience engagement than it is to read years old tweets.

To start, make a list of law firms comparable to yours in both size and client type. Of those on the list, select the firms you respect and research their marketing presence. What channels are they active on? Do they have great, informational content on their website? Compare your strategies with theirs and make plans to incorporate similar tactics into your marketing. Many who want to grow their firm will stop here, but in doing so, they're stopping short of the research that will provide insight on marketing strategies and growth.

In addition to researching similarly situated law firms, you should also research law firms that have experienced the kind of growth you're now seeking. What channels are these firms marketing through? How is the content they generate different from yours? This level of research will provide you with a road map to implement as your law firm grows.

You should look at everything, including the copy, the graphics, the video quality, and the landing pages. What do they do that leads to success? I am not saying to copy it word for word, but definitely use it for inspiration. Your ads will be based on your message and brand. That is what makes you unique.

Where Is Your Audience?

Perhaps the most recurrent question in marketing strategies is, "Do you know who your audience is?" We revisit this question repeatedly because you can't convey a marketing message if you don't know who you're conveying the message to. In addition to the question of "who," you need to know where your audience is. Your answer to the "where" question has to be more specific than "online." You need to know what channels they're using and even when they're most likely to be in those channels. You also need to know what type of content they are consuming. If you have an audience that consumes memes, your ads may need to be more meme-driven. If you have an audience that consumes longform videos or instructional videos, you should be sure to deliver that type of content to them.

Different demographics will seek out information in different places. Some demographics are apt to spend more time in front of their television than online, for example. To examine further, older demographics who spend time on social media platforms are more likely to be Facebook users than TikTok users. Still, if your firm focuses on the defense of college-age students in disciplinary matters, you will find more success on

Instagram or Twitter than you will on LinkedIn or the radio. If your practice concentrates on business law, you may find your clients are particularly adept at networking and place high a value on word-of-mouth referrals.

> ## You can't convey a marketing message if you don't know who you're conveying the message to.

I'll break down the most popular marketing channels in subsequent chapters. In this chapter, it's important to understand the big picture significance of the marketing channel as it relates to your marketing campaign. To drive home the point: marketing channels are pathways to your audience, and without these channels, there is no marketing campaign.

Consider Your Ability to Scale Before Launching on Numerous Channels

Effective marketing is a beautiful thing, and it's the number one way you'll grow your law firm into an 8 Figure Firm. That's why it can be hard for motivated individuals to pump the breaks on their marketing when the campaigns are going really well or when they have really great ideas. In today's tech world, it's easier than ever to reach thousands of potential clients with just a few clicks, so why wouldn't you send your marketing messages out on every available platform? Before committing to a huge, multi-channel marketing campaign, you need to ask yourself if you're ready to grow.

The answer to this question lies in your preparation. Do you have a business plan? Do you have a budget? Do you have company goals for the year? Is your marketing consistent with those goals? Do you have quarterly initiatives? Does your firm know your brand appeal and your message? Can they recite it to clients and potential clients? Do you have the space for new hires? Have you developed a hiring plan?

If you answer yes to all of these questions, you are ready to scale your business and your marketing. Failure to say yes to each question will create inefficiency in your efforts and result in a lot of waste.

I recently spoke with a client who was in the growth mode but wanted to take her law firm to another level. She had grown from $1.5 million in revenue to $2.4 million in revenue. She was understaffed, overworked, and felt like she was spinning her wheels. Naturally, on our introduction call I asked her the questions above. She said no to more than 50 percent of the questions. That was the problem. We immediately started working on getting all of the key areas fixed. Less than 30 days later we heard the bad news.

Here was the bad news: in the past 24 months, because of a failure to plan properly and be properly staffed during her growth period, she had missed out on an estimated five new clients per week.

For those of you who aren't good at math, that's 260 new clients per year and 520 new clients over a two-year period. She had missed them because she did not follow up with leads, scheduled leads for weeks out from the initial call, and was taking months to do work that should have only taken weeks to do. Yet she had managed to grow to $2.4 million because she had tremendous charisma.

To make matters more painful, we multiplied the lost clients by her average case value of $7,000 and we soon realized we had missed $3,640,000 in revenue! Ouch!!!

Before you go into the scaling mode you have to be prepared for the scale.

The Pitfalls of Growing Too Fast Too Soon

Great marketing results in huge growth, and even though this is a book dedicated to helping you grow your firm immensely, there are some important caveats. Too much growth, when you're unprepared for it, can backfire and leave you understaffed. When law firms experience an influx of new clients without adequate infrastructure, work quality can suffer. Clients will start to use your marketing channels against you. Those who've had a bad experience with your firm won't hesitate to leave bad Google reviews or comments on your social media pages, and clients who feel like they haven't received the kind of attention their legal matter deserves certainly won't recommend your firm to their friends, family, or professional network. The worst-case scenario could even be a malpractice suit.

The good news is that solid marketing strategies really do work, but it's advisable to incrementally expand your operative channels so you can adjust to the influx of new clients accordingly. Measured marketing campaigns can provide insight into predictable growth patterns over time, and once you have enough data to extrapolate your growth predictions, you can expand accordingly. And predictability is the name of the game. In fact, I would argue it is more important than revenue growth.

Allocating Your Marketing Budget to Channels

The costs of implementing your marketing campaign through various channels will depend on numerous factors, including the size of the campaign and how much of the process you plan to outsource. Importantly, there are also costs associated with in-house marketing work because every hour you or an employee spends on marketing is an hour not spent on client billing. This isn't to say it's not worth it, and in fact, it absolutely is when done correctly. Understanding the allocation of your marketing budget to various channels is important for a couple of reasons. You'll avoid breaking the bank, and you'll also be able to better gauge your return on investment, allowing for a deep understanding of what strategies are or aren't working for you.

So, what should your budget actually look like if applied to common marketing channels? In the examples below, let's assume the following starting point based on reinvesting 25 percent of your annual revenue into your marketing:

- Annual revenue of previous year: $3 million

- Annual marketing budget in the new year: $750,000

Example No. 1: Referral Channels/Customer Journey

A great baseline target allocation for your referral channels is five percent of your entire marketing budget. Using the assumed numbers listed above, you would put $37,500 into your referral channels marketing. Considering how critical referrals are to new client acquisition, five percent could seem like a dismal budget, but referrals are comparatively low-cost channels to begin with. This is one reason we love referrals! Referrals are free in some ways, but costs are associated with building and maintaining relationships behind the scenes.

Example No. 2: Organic Social Media Channels

Five percent, or $37,500 of your entire marketing budget, is also a great starting allocation for organic social media channels. The costs associated with organic social media pertain to personnel costs and content creation costs, but the posts themselves don't cost anything.

Example No. 3: Paid Social Media

Paid social media channels require the same prep work as organic social media, with the added costs of paying for the platform to boost the post. This is why 10 percent of your annual marketing budget is a safe place to start. In our example, this is about $75,000.

The examples above aren't the only areas your marketing budget will fund, but they are some of the most effective marketing channels used by law firms today. The rest of your marketing budget will be allocated to marketing strategies associated with the overarching marketing campaigns, like search engine optimization (10 percent), pay-per-click marketing (10 percent), and branding (60 percent).

Sample Marketing Budget and Plan on $500,000 Marketing Spend

<u>Marketing Budget</u>

XXXXXXXXXXXX Law's revenue goal for 2022 will be $4,000,000. As of October 2021, the marketing budget is $170,254 to date. Our goal will be to increase the marketing budget to $500,000 for the fiscal year of 2022, which represents 25 percent of last year's revenue. This will be accomplished the following way:

1. Marketing budget should be allocated:

2. The money should be divided the following way with the different marketing channels:

   a. Facebook

      $10,000 per month on paid spend

   b. PPC

      $5,000 per month

c. SEO

$5,000 per month

d. Content Creation

$7,000 per month

e. TV

$10,000 per month

f. Marketing Agency

$3,000 per month

g. Radio

$600 per month

h. Billboard

$3,500 per month

i. Customer Journey

$3,000 per month

j. Client Swag

$800 per month

The plan above yielded $4.2 million in revenue. I am not saying this plan will work for you, but it is a good guideline to study.

Track Trends and Reallocate Your Marketing Budget as Needed

Colin Powell is credited with saying, "There are no secrets to success. It is the result of preparation, hard work, and learning from failure." Regardless of where you are in your marketing journey, you'll make mistakes every now and then.

However, as the quote implies, success is a byproduct of planning, working, and overcoming mistakes. Mistakes, or even the chance of mistake, can be a difficult pill for the risk-averse to swallow, but the entrepreneur knows the value of learning lessons. 8 Figure Firm managers are entrepreneurs!

Figuring out which marketing channels work best for you can present a learning curve, but you'll soon learn what works best for you through careful tracking and adjusting. You'll make mistakes along the way, but below are some tips that may help you avoid some common errors.

- **Tip No. 1: Stay flexible with your budget.** While I've included some baseline numbers in this book to work as examples, you may need to adjust your budget based on your firm's circumstances or client preferences. Guidelines are not the gospels. Allow grace in the execution of your plan. Sometimes the numbers will be off a bit, and that is ok. If you go over on your spend for a channel or for a strategy, don't stress. Try to find out how to get it back in balance in the next quarter. Your goal is to keep your entire strategy at 25 percent for the year. The percentage will fluctuate throughout the year as your revenues rise and fall.

- **Tip No. 2: Spend some time developing an understanding of platform metrics.** Deciphering costs per click (CPCs), click-through rates (CTRs), conversion rates (CVRs), and costs per acquisition (CPA) are all metrics that can help you determine how effective your marketing campaign has been. Even when you outsource your marketing, it's helpful to have a working knowledge of the terms and their significance. I discuss some of the more common terms later in this book.

- You are ultimately responsible for the success of your marketing, not your vendors. Stop relying on them telling you if you are succeeding or not. Know how to calculate the ROI on your investment. Remember that as your marketing spend grows, direct attribution will be harder and harder to determine. Do not focus on direct attribution as the exclusive metric for the success of your channels. Look at the global cost of acquisition. Branding will make it virtually impossible to determine where cases come from. The key is to get cases at less than the diminishing return number.

- **Tip No. 3: Use third-party analytics, like Google, to track performance across marketing channels.** While you can use individual platform analytics to track performance within the platform, third-party analytics will provide you with a big picture understanding of how those platforms are performing compared to one another.

- Keep in mind that these metric tools are only guides. What ultimately matters is how your marketing is performing overall, not just based on one metric.

- **Tip No. 4: Understand that different marketing channels may be significant at different times in the customer journey and consider this in your performance analysis.** You might generate more leads from Facebook but ultimately gain more conversions from LinkedIn. If LinkedIn shows less engagement than Facebook, it doesn't necessarily mean LinkedIn is underperforming.

- There will be times where you are in awareness mode, and you may want to focus on creating the maximum awareness possible. Other times you will want to focus on building your reputation. And yet other times you will want to focus on sales. The purpose of your campaigns will depend on how you view the return on investment. Every investment into marketing cannot be sales-based. Sometimes creating the awareness will be foundational to your sales tactics later in the future.

- **Tip No. 5: Include a call to action (CTA) in posts across all platforms.** A CTA such as "Contact us now to learn how our firm can help you today" may seem trivial, but the CTA is a critical step that moves a potential client through a conversion step.

As you move through the process of determining which marketing channels work best for your firm and at which stage of the marketing campaign the channels are most effective, you'll be able to ascertain where your budget is best applied. Be sure you focus on building marketing campaigns that target your key client and surround them with marketing where the client is found. Do not just blindly market using a channel that someone else uses just because it works for them. Do what works for you by knowing your audience and communicating a clear message and brand.

CHAPTER 7

MANAGING MARKETING FUNNELS

"The first rule of any technology used in business is that automation applied to an efficient operation will magnify the efficiency. The second is that automation applied to an inefficient operation will magnify the inefficiency."

Bill Gates

Before I get into the various methods of marketing your law firm, we should discuss a few tools and concepts that will help you organize your processes. Law firm managers working on exploding the growth of their firm should understand the need for organization and efficiency in moving forward. You'll need both if you plan to ramp up marketing, and then you'll need them again when you are ultimately successful in finding the kind of growth you're aiming for. Scaling is no small task, yet it is a requirement for staying at the top of the game.

In terms of marketing, it's key to understand what the marketing funnel is and how it works. As the name implies, the marketing funnel is a term to describe the way a customer is channeled from their initial awareness of your firm through to their decision to pay you for your services. The wide top of the funnel represents a prospective client's broad and perhaps general understanding of your existence, down to the narrower belief that they do, in fact, need your law firm to help them with their legal issues.

From the widest section of the funnel down to the narrowest, the customer progresses through the following stages:

1. Awareness

2. Interest

3. Consideration

4. Conversion

The funnel can be assigned more specifically once you've honed your customer personas, as discussed in the previous chapter, but the four stages described here represent a broad approach to understanding how the marketing funnel works. To watch one lead work through their individual marketing funnel could look something like this: Someone is injured in a car accident in Memphis, and they feel they need an attorney, so they Google "car wreck lawyer in Memphis."

1. *Awareness*—You regularly post blog articles and videos on your firm's website discussing the legalities of car accidents in Memphis, so your web page pops up in the person's search because you utilize keywords and Search Engine Optimization (SEO).

2. *Interests*—The injured person clicks on your page and explores your blog postings and attorney bios.

3. *Consideration*—A chat bot pops up while the person is perusing your webpage and asks them if they'd like a

free consultation. The person fills out the contact sheet; after all, they do need an attorney, and your firm showcases your experience and know-how.

4. *Conversion*—You reach out directly to the person and give them a pitch that weighs their needs and the value you can offer. They hire you to represent them in their car accident claim.

This is a very simplistic explanation of this process. The process can actually be more involved and more complex and probably should be. When you are creating momentum at the beginning of the funnel you should be aiming to create as much awareness as you possibly can. The name of the game in scaling your law firm is impressions. Never forget what I said at the beginning of the book: people are predictable. Use that predictability to showcase how wonderful your law firm is as much as possible. Awareness leads to impressions, and impressions result in leads. What kind of leads? Leads that are attracted to your brand appeal. And your brand appeal comes from intangibles such as who you are, what you look like, and how you present yourself plus your message. I hope you see how all of this works together.

By the time the lead makes it through the funnel to the conversion stage, they know what you have to offer, and you know what they need with specificity. It seems like a fairly intuitive progression, right? While somewhat organic, a considerable amount of marketing legwork still goes into funneling a lead from awareness through to conversion—not the least of which was that blog post or video that initially piqued the potential client's interest.

From the top of the funnel to the bottom, the client encountered numerous touchpoints that needed to be efficiently managed. So how do you handle each touchpoint for each lead? Enter CRM—which is short for customer relationship management.

The name of the game in scaling your law firm is impressions.

Embrace Customer Relationship Management

There are many ways to describe what CRM is, and Salesforce does it well: "When people talk about CRM, they are usually referring to a CRM system, a tool that helps with contact management, sales management, agent productivity, and more. CRM tools can now be used to manage customer relationships across the entire customer lifecycle, spanning marketing, sales, digital commerce, and customer service interactions."

CRM is vital to your customer acquisition and retention success because it allows you to automate the management of customer relationships. It's not uncommon for attorneys to think this tool is overkill. You made it through law school, the bar exam, the grueling work environment, and you're even spearheading your firm's marketing campaign. You can do it all, so why do you need CRM software? Well, the answer is simple. The point of building an 8 Figure Firm isn't to work yourself into the ground, remember? You want to build a business that generates significant income without you having to have your hand on the wheel of each component, no matter how small. It may seem manageable now, but to get to eight figures, you need significantly more clients. When you have exponential client growth, your ability to scale will hinge on how openly you embrace CRM and how effectively you use it. As my law firm continues to surpass the 10,000 lead level, it is easy to see why I would need a CRM. However, sometimes it is much more difficult to see this when the lead level is at 20 per month. I want to caution you against that thinking. No matter the amount of leads you are receiving, it is important that you maintain them in a system where you can track the status and the follow up process in an orderly way.

Without CRM software as a centralized point of data storage, you risk losing notes and ideas, which translates into losing at least some of the time and resources spent acquiring that information. Not only will CRM software store this information for you, but it will also help you synthesize it into reports that, when created manually, would eat up your time or the time of whoever you've delegated the task to.

There are various CRM products geared specifically toward law firm management and choosing what works best for you and your growth goals is specific to each firm. Notably, your primary CRM could and probably should be coupled with a service like Hootsuite that auto schedules and posts to your social media business pages.

Ultimately, you should look for CRM software that allows you to:

- Create and track client persona segmentation
- Manage and automate client communication
- Sort client data with specified criteria
- Easily update client records

I see a lot of attorneys who already have CRM software and find it beneficial in one way or another but aren't taking full advantage of everything the product has to offer. This approach makes me think about someone who gets up to adjust the volume on their TV even though the remote control is sitting right next to them. It's there for a reason; why not use it? At the end of the day, your primary goal is to stoke the fires of firm growth to new heights, and unless you are utilizing the tools available to you in the most effective and efficient ways, you'll be making it much more difficult than it needs to be. The learning curve for new software and tech can be an obstacle, but it's always worth it in the long term.

CHAPTER 8

REFERRALS: THE LIFEBLOOD OF THE BUSINESS

"A trusted referral is the holy grail of advertising."

Mark Zuckerberg

Without referrals, it is impossible to sustain your business long-term. The cost of acquisition for clients is growing every single year. And the competition is becoming more fierce. For this reason, you must rely on referrals to lower the cost of acquisition and increase your base. Referrals are an indication that your business is providing good customer service. A failure to develop referrals is evidence that you are not committed to your customer journey and the experience that the client has while working with your firm. If you want to create more referrals, you have to be intentional about referral development. You will naturally gain referrals by working through your customer journey. But that is not the only way that you can develop referrals.

Three Types of Referrals

There are three principal types of referrals that you want to be working intentionally to create.

The first type of referral is obvious. That is a referral that comes from another attorney. As obvious as this may sound, I'm surprised when I hear of lawyers who have never networked with other lawyers to develop a referral strategy. If you are a family lawyer, you should do everything within your power to be on the referral list for large personal injury firms in your community. Having a firm that generates close to 13,000 leads per year, we invariably receive family law-type cases every single day. If it were not for the relationships that we have built with family lawyers, we would not have anyone to refer to. For this reason, we have developed a list of family lawyers to whom we refer based upon geographic location in the city of Atlanta. And so, if you are a family lawyer, you should be networking with personal injury lawyers so that you can be on their list.

If you're a personal injury lawyer, you should be working to be on the list of every law firm that does not do personal injury. One of the things that I have found over the years is that many non-personal injury lawyers will advertise for accident cases. The reason for this is that these personal injury cases tend to have high values and many non-personal injury law firms want to be able to refer these cases to specialized attorneys. Having a referral relationship with lawyers who do not practice personal injury is the greatest way to guarantee that those lawyers will refer business to you.

The second type of referral is a referral that comes from non-lawyer professionals. Non-lawyer professionals such as your barber, your insurance agent, your primary care doctor, your dentist, etc. all play an integral part in the development of your business. Although they may not know it, they will be a valuable resource to you. When I started the Scott law firm I knew that I needed to spend a lot of time networking and building relationships. Instead of staying in my office and grinding, I spent a lot of time outside of the office going to places where I thought my clients would be. In that process I had my banker send me three new cases. I had my barber send me two or three new cases. I had my insurance agent send me two or three new cases. I then went and networked with chiropractors who sent me six to eight new cases. None of this networking led to immediate results for me because I was doing contingency work. What it did do is lead me to the belief that I would be able to survive if I could just hold on until the day that the cases started settling.

What I realized is that even though it's so important to reach out to lawyer professionals who have the contacts already, reaching out to non-lawyer professionals who are engaged in the community and may know people who have your particular case type was supremely beneficial. For this reason, I spent a lot of time with non-lawyer professionals and suggest that you do the same.

It is my recommendation that if you are starting off as a personal injury lawyer, you spend the first three to five months of your business generating referrals by meeting new chiropractors. A couple of years ago, before the pandemic hit, I went down to Savannah, Georgia, where I was making an attempt to expand our office. In that attempt I was able to meet six to eight doctors and have lunch and dinner with them so I could gauge their interest in working with our law firm. Within less than 30 days one of the doctors that I had met on that Savannah trip became a great ally. That one doctor alone sent me nine cases In the first 30 days. Do not underestimate the power of building referral relationships with non-lawyer professionals.

The third and last group of people you should be developing relationships with in order to develop referrals is your clients themselves. Have you asked your client for a reference? have you asked your client for a review? Have you asked your client to be your advocate? Client referral-building is the easiest of the three types of referral relationships because you already have a relationship with the person you're asking for a referral from. One of the things that I like to do is ask for a referral. I don't wait around until the client decides that they want to give me a referral. I tried to find points of happiness to then ask the client if they would be willing to send me a new client. This strategy ensures that you're catching the client during the highest period of their relationship with you.

Understanding the customer journey can feel like trying to hit a moving target, and if you plan to wait until you've fully grasped it, you may find yourself stuck. There will come a time when you must move forward in the execution of your plan. If you've completed the steps of building insight into the customer journey, you're ready to wade into the methods of marketing that will work best for your firm. The type of advertising you do will ultimately depend on your budget, at least at first, and who your customers are. It will look different for each firm, and you should be prepared to get it wrong at least some of the time. Advertising available to law firms falls primarily into one of three big umbrella categories: referrals, digital (including social media), and mass media.

Law firm management and ownership is an industry in and of itself. Yes, your job as an attorney is to provide excellent legal services to your clients, but if you want an 8 Figure Firm, you have to embrace the business end of it and understand how to do what your competitors are doing. Then you need to do it better. Referrals are the bread and butter of most successful law firm marketing strategies because they're an investment return on all of your prior sales efforts and on a legal job well done. Referrals don't cost you anything on top of what you've already put into attracting and retaining the client. An added bonus is that even firms with less-developed marketing budgets can reap the massive benefits of word-of-mouth marketing.

On top of the cost benefits to you, referral marketing is extremely productive. Nielson reports eight out of 10 customers worldwide value and trust word-of-mouth recommendations more than any other source. Two-thirds of those surveyed report the referral doesn't always need to come directly from their inner circle—an online customer shoutout from an unknown individual will also invoke a level of brand trust.

> **Referrals are the bread and butter of most successful law firm marketing strategies because they're an investment return on all of your prior sales efforts and on a legal job well done.**

While referral marketing can happen organically, it doesn't happen enough. That said, there are strategies and practices you can implement to boost referrals. Clients, colleagues, and others in your community will inevitably forget to pass along their recommendations because, well, life is busy. In fact, while a significant number of potential referrals would be ready and willing to tell another person about you, less than one-third of them actually do because it simply slips their mind.

I've had my own friends and family fail to refer business to me and then tell me they were not thinking about it when they heard of the case.

So, how do you boost referrals for your firm? We'll look at the three most common areas of referral marketing for lawyers. Outside of friends, family, and your day-to-day contacts, referrals are nearly always going to come from the following sources:

1. Clients

2. Other Attorneys

3. Non-Attorney Professionals

While the name of the game is the same for each referral source, you ultimately need to go about incentivizing the referrals differently. Additionally, there are certain pitfalls specific to each category that you need to be on the lookout for.

Referrals from Clients

Clients make excellent referral sources. Their family and friends know that the referral comes from a place of trust, and they are apt to put their faith in the recommendation. These referrals can occur in different ways, and you should do everything possible to secure them.

1. Organic Client Referrals

Client referrals can happen organically, and many firms rely on the fact that their good work and above-par customer service will generate new leads. After all, individuals who run in the same professional or socioeconomic groups tend to have the same legal troubles. Doctors who need malpractice defense will know other doctors who need malpractice defense. Real estate agents who need to resolve title disputes have colleagues and clients with the same legal issues. If you do your job well, you're more likely to get referrals—the key to procuring those coveted and organically manifested client referrals is to go above and beyond customer expectations.

These naturally occurring client referrals are great, but unfortunately, they don't happen nearly as often as they could. The good news is it's relatively simple to ramp up your client referral marketing if you act with intentionality. The secret is in the ask. Ask for more referrals from your clients, and you will get them.

2. How to Boost Client Referrals

Planting the seed of referral in your clients begins long before you wrap up your case or project for them. It begins with their customer journey and proceeds through each touchpoint along the way. One thing I like to do when working with my clients is to tell them that I plan to ask them for a referral on day one.

The Script for the Ask

"Hey John, I just wanted to thank you again for trusting me to help you in your case. As the case goes along, my plan is to ask you to refer any person to me that may have a similar case. I hope that our relationship continues to develop so that you have the trust and confidence in me to refer someone to me. I know I need to get you results and I am committed to making that happen. That is why I am not going to ask for a referral at this time. But my firm thrives on referrals so it is likely that I or my legal assistant will reach out throughout the representation. If you ever feel that I haven't done enough to earn a referral from you, my hope is that you let me know so that I can deliver on any promises I have made in the representation."

This script above has planted enough seeds that it has generated more than $20,000,000 in referrals in my last 15 years in the legal profession.

Competent legal representation will only take you so far when it comes to client referrals. To maximize your referral marketing, you also need nail customer service. Customer service opportunities for law firm offices abound. From quickly responding to emails and phone calls to offering refreshments while a client waits for a meeting—*every* interaction with a customer is an opportunity for customer service. While the sky's the limit, don't forget that it's often the small, intangible actions that move mountains. Did a client have a baby? Send a card. Did a client suffer a setback? Send flowers. When clients feel like your firm is family, they'll tell their family about your firm. My dad has always told me that you cannot outspend generosity. Of course, this doesn't mean that you should be reckless in your customer service but look to wow and delight your clients and the return will be exponential.

You should also provide tools for your clients to promote you more effectively. Remember—out of sight, out of mind. Newsletters and blogs are excellent tools that make your content easily shareable. Videos explaining the next step in the process have also been highly effective for both consumer and business law. You can also ask clients to share a review of your services on Google, Yelp, or your website. Let all of your clients know that if they refer people to you, they will receive a discounted rate or a lowered contingency fee. It's ok to sweeten the pot so long as you comply with the ethical guidelines in your jurisdiction.

Here's one particularly potent trick of the trade I've learned—don't write off a client with whom you've made mistakes. A client who sees accountability through an above and beyond effort to "make things right" will return their loyalty to you tenfold. Let's face it, lawyers have a reputation, and when you do all that's in your power to convey humanity and earnest advocacy, the client will remember it. And they will tell their friends.

3. Avoiding Client Referral Pitfalls

It's natural for a client who's built a trusted relationship with a specific attorney at your law firm to only recommend that attorney to their friends. You're likely to find that this repeatedly happens, creating a difficult bottleneck situation. This will happen when your referrals all go to the same one or two lawyers. While it's great that the referral marketing is generating new leads, you need to distribute the work among all attorneys as much as is practicable. One way to overcome this hurdle is to focus your referral marketing on your law firm brand rather than individual attorneys. To do so, you can leverage paralegals and support staff who work across multiple attorneys so that your clients will see familiar faces consistently, no matter who handles their case. Although I want to promote my attorneys as much as possible because they are part of the fabric of the brand. I want to make sure that we are pushing the fullness of the business in our referral strategy. It's no different than a sports team: you must promote the team and not just the players.

Another roadblock may arise if your support staff isn't willing to play for the team. Even when a client receives rockstar legal services, they may forego recommending your firm to their friends and family if their interactions with your support staff were unpleasant or if they had to wait longer than they felt was reasonable for a return call or other administrative resolution. Make sure every law firm employee understands that they are the face of your firm when they interact with clients.

A client who sees accountability through an above and beyond effort to "make things right" will return their loyalty to you tenfold.

Referrals from Other Lawyers

In many ways, lawyers practicing at other firms within your area are in an even better position to provide referrals for your services than a layperson client is. When a lawyer gives a referral, potential clients rightfully perceive elevated credibility. These referrals may even come from competitor law firms—an important incentive to practice civility even in an adversarial profession. When receiving referrals from lawyers, it is critical that you meet the expectations of the referring lawyer.

At our firm, we have a list of attorneys to whom we refer clients. For us, it is a deal breaker if the lawyer we refer business to does not meet the quality of representation or customer services that we provide. The reason for this standard is that a referral reflects the value we perceive in others and the perception is that it is also the value that we provide. We do not want to send mixed messages in the referral handoff.

1. Organic Lawyer-to-Lawyer Referrals

Most successful law practices provide services within a specific legal niche—they are the experts in their field. That said, the general public will never quite understand this, and every lawyer you know has had a family member ask them for help with a legal matter completely unrelated to the type of law the attorney practices. When this happens, and it always happens, that lawyer will often refer their friends and family to someone better equipped to handle their case. Despite all of our efforts to brand our firm as an "accident and injury" law firm, we receive hundreds of leads every single month with clients asking for legal services unrelated to what we do. In some months we may receive over 100 leads for an unrelated practice area.

It's also not uncommon for lawyers to refer their clients to other attorneys when a different type of expertise is needed. For instance, a criminal defense lawyer is apt to get an estate planning question from their long-term client or someone their client referred. Most attorneys will point the individual in the direction of another lawyer who can adequately handle the case. Ironically, even attorneys and law firms in direct competition will often refer clients to one other when a conflict of interest prevents a firm from taking on an individual's case. In his book *Leads to Referrals*, Timothy M. Houston writes, "The smart business person sees an opportunity to generate referrals by collaborating with their competitors."

This is another area where we excel. Although we do injury law, we have routinely referred complex cases to competitors or specialized lawyers who may have a different perspective on a particular type of case. As we have grown, we have also become the go-to law firm for cases referred from out of state. Our list of cases referred from lawyers from out of state has now grown to the hundreds because we network with lawyers consistently.

Attorneys will have a more sophisticated understanding of what makes you and your firm a possible referral. After all, they're vying for their own referrals, and they're hoping the client will ultimately come back to them when the services they offer fit the needs of the client. Those attorneys, if they're smart, won't jeopardize their reputation by sending potential future clients to unreliable attorneys. The key to successfully obtaining organic lawyer-to-lawyer referrals is your reputation and your visibility. That is to say, other firms need to know who you are, and they need to trust you.

2. How to Boost Lawyer-to-Lawyer Referrals

Lawyer-to-lawyer referrals are usually handled in a very lawyerly manner. They often grow out of interactions during business development opportunities, courthouse interactions, or continued learning events. Generally, lawyers practice some form of reciprocity when referring clients to each other, and the more skillfully you navigate this process, the more easily you'll win those referrals. As with clients, your journey to lawyer referrals is a process. You don't want to cold-call other lawyers in your city and bluntly ask for referrals—instead, you develop a relationship with the other attorneys. Call them and ask if they'd like to grab coffee instead. Build a report first, then broach the topic of referrals.

After you make contact, the next task is staying in touch. Business relationships are a lot like any other type of relationship, and they require work. Sometimes the work looks like maintaining an active membership with various organizations, and sometimes it looks like participating in programs put on by your local and state bar associations. Some attorneys keep track of the number of hours they invest in maintaining these relationships—making it a goal to put in four or five hours a week. This is a smart and manageable way to hold yourself accountable to the practice of fostering lawyer-to-lawyer referral relationships. Be sure to have a budget for lawyer referrals and stick to consistently building and cultivating those relationships.

3. Avoiding Lawyer-to-Lawyer Referral Pitfalls

The goal is referrals, but I've seen plenty of attorneys get fouled up when those referrals come to call. For starters, if you've properly developed your lawyer-to-lawyer referral relationships, then those other attorneys should know what your practice area is. If, however, you haven't clearly communicated your expertise, you may end up getting referrals that you can't adequately represent. When you have to turn these potential clients away, you'll find that you start to lose traction with those other lawyers who were so willing to send people your way. This happened to us when we had a referral attorney on our list who did employment law. We had a good relationship and began sending the lawyer cases. After sending almost 100 cases to this lawyer and realizing that he wasn't accepting any case, we called and asked him what was going on. Come to find out he only did federal employment cases. That was a big miss on our part.

Another important thing to touch on is how you handle referral fees. It's not uncommon for attorneys to arrange referral fees, which is ultimately a convenient way to incentivize the funneling of clients to you. While the exchange of referral fees for leads can prove beneficial, you need to make sure you are working within the parameters set by the laws of your state. Additionally, your expectations should be clear and in writing. If you owe a referral fee, pay it. Don't forget that in many jurisdictions, the client must be informed of the referral fee in advance.

Referrals from Non-attorney Professionals

Seeking referrals from other non-attorney professionals provides those benefits I've already mentioned, and the method by which you go about procuring them is also similar. Professional referrals may carry more weight than a referral from a friend or family because, as with lawyer-to lawyer referrals, professionals lend an additional layer of credibility.

1. Organic Referrals from Professionals

Organic referrals from professionals occur in many of the ways already mentioned. Similarly situated people tend to run in the same circles, so if you're already catering to professionally inclined clients, it's likely that you'll see some professional referrals funneled your way.

Any number of day-to-day interactions can lead to professional referrals—don't be shy about letting your doctor, your accountant, your real estate agent, or your dog's veterinarian know that you'd love it if they spread the word about your law firm.

But why stop there?

2. How to Boost Referrals from Professionals

A great strategy for boosting referrals from professionals outside of your immediate legal sphere is to elevate your visibility in the community at large. Professional and community organizations offer numerous opportunities for exposure. Most groups regularly host guest speakers to help inform their members on specific topics, policy changes, or best practices. For example, if your firm focuses on real estate issues, reach out to the National Association of Realtors and local chapters. You can offer to provide insight on recent changes in statutes or interpretations of the law.

Even when you aren't offered an opportunity to speak directly to an audience, the act of sending an email or making a phone inquiry counts as a touchpoint that raises the brand awareness of your firm. Consider that every moment in your life is a potential touchpoint for a lead. You are your own living, breathing touchpoint machine.

3. Avoiding Referrals from Professionals Pitfalls

When you're actively outreaching to community professionals in the hopes of bolstering referral marketing, you must make sure your messaging is clear and geared toward your intended audience. You need to avoid sending the message that you're a jack of all trades when you're, in fact, a mass torts lawyer, but you also don't want to give off an appearance of disorganization or other lack of capability. You should have your pitch ready before you make your first phone call. If you research your audience as you should, then you'll know what they need before you pitch a speaking engagement topic. You need to avoid reaching out if your plan is premature, because that may lead potential clients to think that you are unprepared and don't know or understand their needs.

Managing the Referral Game

Referral marketing is relatively intuitive and accessible to every law firm owner. This is both good news and bad news. It's good news because it means there is no bar to entry; it's bad news because it means if you can do it with ease, so can your competitors. To stay several steps ahead of lawyers competing for the same clients, you need to approach referral marketing with a dynamic strategy.

Remember that customer service and excellent legal services are only the first steps to procuring word-of-mouth leads.

You also need to develop relationships with attorneys from various practice areas, including your own, so they feel comfortable sending clients your way when the occasion arises. Further, stay visible within your target client base through social engagements and community service. While it's easy to practice one or two of these strategies, you should master all of them if you want to excel. This can become a juggling act if you don't approach it with sophisticated attention to detail and manage contacts through your CRM software or other tracking mechanisms.

Currently, 37.7 percent of all clients that hire my firm come by way of referral despite us spending millions of dollars on marketing. If you remember from the earlier chapters, marketing and advertising spending produces width in your business. The depth of your business will come from your customer journey and referral building. This will dramatically drive down the global cost of acquisition and will allow you to sign more cases with your budget than simply relying on one strategy alone. As more and more referral leads hit your office, you must stay organized or you will create a chaotic environment and not provide the customer service you likely desire.

To combat the chaos, utilize an automation system for sending emails and newsletters. Track referral source data in spreadsheets and CRM's, being sure to include helpful resources like contact information and more personal details such as birthdays, job title, etc. When you track the amount of time you've spent with these referral resources and the amount of work generated from each, you can better prioritize the energy spent on each. If, over a two-year period, you've put the same amount of time into two different referral resources and only one of them has produced in a meaningful way, it's time to reallocate your efforts to the more productive source.

Remember that when your referral marketing starts to pay off, you'll need to be able to scale up for the work coming your way. Try to avoid funneling all leads to just a fraction of your attorneys and instead push your law firm brand as a whole. Over time, your referral marketing strategies will pay off, and new referrals will end up becoming sources themselves. The positive feedback loop created by a strategic and successful referral marketing campaign leads to huge growth when you remember the following:

Referrals are the firm's return on marketing and customer service investment. Referrals are a no-cost/low-cost way to generate leads, but that doesn't mean you haven't invested time and resources into earning them. They are the most trusted marketing tool, but they will be generated more easily by established firms than by new firms. Staying visible in your community and establishing processes for following up with referral sources is paramount.

CHAPTER 9

SOCIAL MEDIA

"We have technology, finally, that for the first time in human history allows people to really maintain rich connections with much larger numbers of people."

Pierre Omidyar

Despite all of the energy and effort I put into writing this book and helping you develop a marketing plan that will make you the king of growth in your market, this chapter may be the most important chapter of the book.

Someone recently told me that social media is the future of law firm marketing. I immediately stopped them dead in their tracks and said, "ABSOLUTELY NOT! It is the present."

The future is here. If you are not using social media to leverage your law firm, you are missing out on thousands if not millions of dollars in a new business. Social media is the billboard of today. And because of the nature of the connections, people trust and like you almost instantaneously.

I have to admit, there was a time in my life where I found social media to be fake or disingenuous. To some extent, it is. People will generally post only the highlights of their life. Those who post the negative tend to get shunned. Everyone is competing for attention, and attention they get. My perspective on this issue changed several years ago when I attended a wedding and a person I had never met in my life walked up to me and started asking me about my kids, Rachel, and a recent trip I had gone on. When I asked him (in embarrassment) how we knew each other he said, "I follow you on social media."

I instantly knew there was an opportunity there. If a perfect stranger could walk up to me and feel this comfortable talking to me, it was because he felt a level of trust and connection. What if I leveraged that trust and connection to build a network of business for my law firm and my consulting firm? That is exactly what I did, and it has now earned me more than $3 million in profit in the last two years and rising. Not bad for something that is relatively inexpensive to being with.

The Power of Social Media

Social media as we know it has been around since the early 2000s, but it's worth noting that, technically, it's been around much longer. In fact, some scholars count the first telegraph sent by Samuel Morse in 1844 as an early attempt at the phenomenon. Aptly, the telegraph read "What Have God Wrought?" and in today's globally connected world of viral cat videos and memes, many of us often wonder the same thing. However, social media serves a valuable purpose and ultimately springboards off of Mankind's natural inclination to connect. When you use social media the right way, you develop relationships that lead to business growth. I want to show you how to do this without having to spend millions of dollars on ads.

The Value of Social Media in Law Practice Marketing

When attorneys create social media accounts representing their law firm brand, they get to do several things. They get to tell their story and grow their audience, which leads to relationship building with potential clients. Social media also allows page account holders to track the data analytics of their audience interactions, providing valuable insight into the customer journey as outlined in earlier chapters. Social media platforms like Facebook and Twitter also provide a place for firm owners and managers to connect followers to their more substantive content within the firm's website.

The bottom line is that most people use social media in some form. Avoiding this marketing resource would be like trying to fish on dry land when you're surrounded by an ocean. There is absolutely no doubt that your competitors are utilizing social media, and you should too. The American Bar Association reports that 80 percent of respondents surveyed maintain a marketing presence on social media and that "[a]mong those firms that do use social media, LinkedIn is still the leading platform at 79 percent, followed by Facebook (54 percent), Martindale (38 percent), and Avvo (23 percent)."

The platform that you will use for marketing is dependent on the practice area. I have found that social media and specific tools such as Lives and Reels work infinitely better in some practice areas than others. Recently working with one of my immigration clients, I saw she was Tik Tok famous with millions of views and almost 100,000 followers on Tik Tok. Assessing what platform works best for you is the most important part of this process.

Adapting to Change

Technology has made overwhelming strides since that first telegraph was sent in 1844. Now, social media platforms cycle through evolutionary change with dizzying speed. Remember Myspace? Or Vine? If not, that's ok because they're now obsolete. Not only do platforms evolve rapidly, as is the case with Facebook algorithms, Instagram stories, and even LinkedIn visibility, but new platforms pop up seemingly overnight. One day you're patting yourself on the back for posting your first Instagram story, and the next day everyone is talking about TikTok. Platforms will continue to fall in and out of favor, and it's not uncommon for them to disappear altogether. The remedy to this disruption is developing a strategy that incorporates this ever-evolving digital landscape.

There are a few ways to go about it. You could hire an expert, for example, if your budget allows—someone whose job it is to stay abreast of social medial changes and trends and who understands how to adjust course. If you don't plan to expend resources on a social media expert, though, that's ok. Remember that marketing lends itself to trial and error, and the key to success is learning from mistakes. The same is true with social media—create your posts and share your content, then review the analytics and see what's generating the most audience interaction. Then, try a new direction and repeat the process. The most important thing to remember in social media marketing is that you have to play the long game.

Organic Social Media

Organic social media is a term that describes the free stuff—the photos, memes, stories, and content that you can share from your business page without paying. Organic posts made by your business page won't have as far a reach as paid advertisements, but they will still reach the audience that has already followed you. If your followers decide to share the post, that reach grows even more. Organic social media allows you to develop your firm's voice and stay connected with your existing followers through curated content that can be helpful, celebratory, or even funny. It's important to note that while you can inject levity and personality into your posts, they should represent the overall integrity of your firm.

The most important thing to remember in social media marketing is that you have to play the long game.

The most successful law firm building you can do is on your personal social media platform, not your business page. Many of the social platforms suppress the business pages unless you spend money on paid ads. If you want people to see and hear you, you have to post on your personal page. My recommendation is that you post at least five times per week on every single platform you can, making the content germane to the specific platform. The content you will post on your personal page will be a mixture of business and pleasure. But be careful not to be overly political or religious. This can work against you in trying to build your business. (It could also work for you if you are only trying to attract clients that agree with your beliefs).

I have found tremendous success in social media posting, especially when the content is funny and engaging. Be yourself. Don't try to be someone else who has a huge following. Your following and engagement come from your authenticity, not from copying what other people do.

The drawback to organic media is that it simply doesn't reach as many people—a fact unlikely to change as the number of voices online continues to grow while attention spans simultaneously diminish. In an article published by Hootsuite, the company notes, "[p]aid and organic social are different beasts best harnessed for different goals." When coupled with paid advertising, organic social media fills the crucial gap between the firm's personality and paid messaging designed to cast a wider net. While investing in paid advertisements is a productive marketing strategy, you can and should leverage organic posts to your marketing advantage as well.

Remember that you are your firm, and your firm is you. As the face of the brand, what you put on your personal page will inform your friends of what type of law firm you run. You may not like that, but it doesn't change it from being true.

Paid Social Media Ads

Ads! Ads! And more Ads! You have to pay to play.

Paying for social media can help boost your audience engagement and your visibility. It's a lot like buying a VIP pass at Disney Land—for a fee, you can pop up to the front of the line. In the case of social media, the front of the line is the top of the feed. With nearly 250 million individuals using social media within the United States, paid ads are the best way to ensure your audience sees your content. If you're going to put the time and energy, perhaps even paying staff to perform social media tasks, you also want to see some return on your investment.

Paid advertising on social media also helps you target your intended audience. Various platforms offer different parameters for filtering through to who sees your ad. Remember that customer persona from earlier in this book? When you choose the filters for your ad, you're recreating that persona within the platform so that your ad caters to, and is streamlined for, the ideal potential client target. The major social media platforms all offer paid advertising options, but you should choose what works best for you and your audience. Remember to play to your strengths, or if possible, outsource the job to experts.

The amount of money that you spend on social media depends largely on what practice area you have. In the personal injury space, you should be ready to drop your kid's college tuition every single month to acquire clients. I say this jokingly but also not really. It is super expensive and competitive to market on social for personal injury.

If, however, you are in a transactional style practice area such as estate planning or even family law, you can generate tons of leads without expending a significant amount of money.

My recommendation is you spend around 10 percent of your budget on paid social media. This spend with a targeted persona, in a specific geo target and with the right message and brand will generate all of the leads you will need to grow your business.

Using this strategy, one of my clients grew from 130 leads per month to over 400 leads per month in less than eight months. Better yet, she doubled her revenues in the same time period while admittedly still leaving leads on the table because the sales team was having some trouble converting. I think she could have tripled her revenues. Nevertheless, the strategy works if you have the right spend, the right message and the right brand.

Facebook and Instagram

For purposes of law firm marketing, Facebook and Instagram advertisements can accomplish two major objectives. First, they can help you build awareness. Second, they foster consideration—meaning the ads will direct traffic to your website and generate communication with you via direct message, comments, or the tried-and-true phone call. Both platforms are owned by Facebook, but the Facebook site offers more ad types than Instagram. Many of Facebook's ad options aren't particularly useful for law firms. For example, lawyers won't generate many viable leads through a playable ad—a mobile-only feature that teases a preview of a game or app. Primarily, photo and video ads will be your most appropriate choice. That said, if you have an original idea that may work well with a carousel ad, give it a try and track the data analytics to see how it lands.

Before planning your strategy, you should have an understanding of your budget. The cost of Facebook advertising, at least at the time of this writing, is described by the company as: "[y]ou tell Facebook how much you want to spend on advertising. Then we'll try to get you as many results as possible for that amount. If you want to spend $5 a week, you can. If you want to spend $50,000 a week, you can do that too." Ultimately, the cost of ads correlates with how beneficial they are to you. For example, an ad that brings awareness is less expensive than one that leads to consideration (i.e., the click of a mouse). This is also known as Pay-Per-Click advertising, as you're charged for what and how your audience engages with your content. Instagram and Facebook use the same Ads Manager, but it's worth noting that Facebook has more data because it's been around much longer. Still, when used effectively, Instagram ads tend to receive nearly 25 percent more engagement.

Before launching a social media campaign, ask yourself what your goals are and set realistic and achievable expectations that can be met within a certain timeframe. The more specific you are, the easier it will be for you to identify and outline your parameters. Once you've made a plan, you need to decide what your ads will look like. Keep in mind that in today's on-the-go culture, most social media users access platforms through their mobile phones. Successful ads will be clear, concise, and designed so someone can get the gist of the message, and perhaps bookmark the content, while they're on the go.

Your posts should also include a call to action, which lets the audience know what the next step is. Calls to action vary, but for law firms, calls to action in a social media advertisement will generally look like:

- Instructing the reader to click for more information

- Asking the reader to "like" the post
- Requesting the reader to read the attached blog
- Asking the reader to register for educational content

The most successful ads will follow these guidelines while also offering relevant and useful information. There are a lot of decisions to make when determining where to advertise and what form your ads should take. I'll remind you that this process requires the acceptance of trial and error and the inevitable failure here and there. If you don't plan to hire a pro, then play to your strengths. Sure, maybe Instagram could lead to more audience engagement, but if you're more efficient with Facebook, then focus your energies there.

Finally, be sure to map out where your client goes when they engage with your content. Will you be sending them to a funnel page, a landing page, your main website, or a lead generation form? All of this matters because this will determine how you will actually get the client on the phone and speak to them about the service and product you are providing. Do not, I repeat, do not just place an ad and expect sales to come in. There has to be an intentional roadmap for the client and a process for aggressively reaching out to each one of those leads.

For 8 Figure, we currently have all leads drop into our CRM, which initiates a series of email communications. They land in our CRM in three different ways: 1. They download my ebook, 2. They fill out a contact us form 3. They send a direct message asking for more information. In addition to the automated communications, one of our sales associates reaches out with a personalized email and text. The person is now in our customer journey.

A Note on LinkedIn for B2B Advertising

While Facebook and Instagram and other social media counterparts are great tools for connecting with a lay audience, they aren't the most effective ways to elevate your B2B marketing. If, for example, your firm specializes in consumer protection defense law and you need to attract auto dealerships or manufacturers as clients to your firm, then LinkedIn will generate more appropriate leads. LinkedIn offers a professional, sophisticated setting for those companies that you'd like to bring on board as clients. Many of the same rules apply— LinkedIn ads should be relevant and informational, and should also close with a call to action. They should also illustrate your expertise and ability to speak with authority in the area of law you practice. With B2B marketing, you need to ramp up the industry lingo, and LinkedIn is the appropriate place to do so. It's also helpful that the Ads Manager used by LinkedIn is similar to the other social network platforms, and your campaign can be run on a modest budget if need be.

LinkedIn is for business professionals, and your paid advertisements can target entire companies or professionals who hold specific job titles, education, or skillsets. You can exclude the same to refine your parameters further. As with the other platforms, LinkedIn ad campaign success will hinge on how well you track your successes or failures and then move forward with that information. Always adapt your strategy to what's working and what isn't.

Twitter and TikTok for Quick Content

Certain social media platforms are adept at sending brief and punchy messaging to your audience. TikTok is still relatively new, but it's nonetheless taken the digital world by storm through short-form mobile videos limited to 15 seconds in length. Though you've probably heard of TikTok in the context of viral dance challenges, it can also be a way to reach an audience with brief, engaging information. For now, the platform is used by a mostly younger audience—think college-age and younger. Still, lawyers like Ethen Ostroff, aka "The TikTok Lawyer," have amassed a huge following by offering short soundbites that answer legal questions. Sometimes the questions are common, and sometimes they are goofy—such as one question regarding whether or not you can bring a lawsuit against NASA if you get hit by space junk. Personality really shines through on TikTok, and while it may not be for every lawyer, don't summarily discount it.

Similarly, Twitter offers an opportunity to share quick-witted insights in 280 characters or less. The hashtag is a prevalent tool of the Twitter trade, and you can stay up to date on real-time trends by following hashtags and sharing information as it happens. On Twitter, the more you engage with individuals, the more prevalent your content will be in their feeds.

YouTube, Blogs, & Podcasts for Long-Form Content

I am a big fan of YouTube. Like, a big fan. If you want to put out some great long-form content and then link it on your website followed up with sharing snippets from the content, YouTube is the place to go. More and more people are getting their information from YouTube. Anything you want to know how to do can be found on this platform. Your content here should not just be instruction but rather how to do something. Be generous with the content and of course do not forget the disclaimers.

If you are a family lawyer, show someone how to fill out the pro se forms for an uncontested divorce. Immigration? They have more forms than any practice area I know. Personal injury? Explain the demand process.

Be sure to simplify the process, but don't explain so much where you are giving a dissertation. You want to give them value but have them simultaneously realize they should be hiring you for the job.

Boosting your videos will also create awareness. Depending on your practice area, it could be much harder to get direct leads from YouTube than other platforms. However, the video content you are creating should be on the platform for purposes of sharing through text and email campaigns.

Popular social media platforms like Facebook, Instagram, and Twitter excel at funneling an audience through to longform content. YouTube, blogs, and podcasts can be as short or long as you want them to be, although in creating them, you need to consider the attention span of your audience. Regardless of the form, longer content should have a purpose, and it should be driven by information you can speak to skillfully. To a certain extent, it should be "evergreen," which is to say you should strive for content that won't be obsolete in a year.

Blogs are a popular tool, not just as law firm website content, but as content offered by any industry professionals across the board. Attending to SEO will further drive leads to your website. The more effective your SEO, the more your website will show up in internet searches. Consider that your audience will probably be using their mobile phones to read your blog. Short chunks of text, four to five lines instead of long blocks, aid mobile readability. SEO can be similarly used in the production of YouTube videos. When a lead enters a search engine query into Google, YouTube videos appear as written content does. Videos should be helpful—consider answering those questions you most often receive from clients, and of course, don't forget your call to action.

Podcasting is a bit of a different beast when it comes to methods of putting content out into the world. Like LinkedIn, podcasts are an effective way to grow your B2B leads through the dissemination of content geared towards professionals with more sophisticated interests in a topic. It's important that you address your audience in a way that demonstrates your expertise and authority. If you have a transactional product, be sure to have a podcast. It has been an incredible tool for getting the credibility of my business out into the world.

Email Campaigns

Email marketing is another way to reach a vast audience with minimal costs. These campaigns can engage current clients and even boost new leads. As with other areas of social media, however, there is a right way and a wrong way to roll out an email campaign. When preparing materials for an email campaign, you need consider who you're targeting and what material you're targeting them with. Sending email content that's uninteresting is tantamount to spam, even if you intend the message to be more meaningful than your recipients find it to be.

Below are some tips for ensuring your email campaign finds a receptive audience:

- Provide succinct, meaningful content

- Send informative content that interests the audience

- Segment your email list so that the appropriate content is sent to an applicable audience

- Don't be afraid to share your thoughts on current legal developments that demonstrate your knowledge and expertise

- Use a combination of video and text copy in emails

- Send at least two emails per week (Yes, you read that right)

The last point really hangs people up. Many lawyers are worried about annoying their audience. I want you to think about this differently. If you went to a concert, would you want the artist to play more songs or fewer songs?

The only people who will be annoyed will be people who find no value in your content. With those people you have two options: create better content or accept that they will likely never be your client so let them unsubscribe. If you are building your email list correctly, you will always add more people to the list than the people that unsubscribe.

Email campaigns are often plagued by the spam folder, but there are some steps you can take to help prevent your emails from ending up forever unread. First, you can ask your audience to add your email to their contact list. Second, make sure the content in your email is free of spelling and grammatical errors; spam filters often flag these issues. Third, use a third-party email marketing program to manage your campaign.

Do not underestimate the compounding effect consistency creates over an extended period of time.

Best Practices – Tips and Strategies

Digital interaction through all social media platforms is often intuitive, but everyone is vulnerable to certain pitfalls that can throw a marketing campaign off course. Below is a list of best practices:

- **Update your social media business pages**. When you change your business contact information, location, or law firm members, let the public know.

- **Keep your personal page messages off your business page.** But use your personal page to promote your business.

- **Think before you post.** Ask yourself if your message shares information of value and if it fits your firm's personality. Ask yourself if a visual aid might drive the point home better than if you posted without any photo. Think about the time of day and consider whether the post may reach more people in an hour or two, or within a few days.

- **Proofread.** Make sure your grammar and spelling are accurate and be sure your message isn't cut off by character limits. Hit them with value in the first two lines of the content. If someone has to hit "read more" to get to the most compelling part of your post, it won't generate as much interest.

- **Be consistent.** Post regularly, at least five times per week. If you find this challenging, check out online resources that will allow you to schedule posts or outsource the task. Play the long game. This is a lifetime effort not a two-month task. Plan to add value for the rest of your life. Do not underestimate the compounding effect consistency creates over an extended period of time.

- **Respond to your audience.** Interacting with followers or potential followers through messaging or by sharing their content is a great way to foster personality and develop relationships.

- **Avoid spamming.** When you share content or post messages, it needs to add value and target an intended audience. Don't send the same carbon copy message to dozens of companies.

- **Handle yourself with grace.** The online world is full of trolls, naysayers, and people just having a bad day. Don't respond reactively, and instead take the high road. Also, be aware that some groups have self-promotion policies; be sure to adhere to group guidelines as it demonstrates a lot about your character, which of course translates as professionalism to potential clients.

Social media is a powerful resource for reaching a lot of people in a short amount of time. What makes it great is that it's available to every law firm owner and fits well within a variety of budgets. Adaptability is key in winning the social media game, but for every change to the algorithm or new platform that emerges, there will be online resources to explain it. Research changes often. To get started, just begin with the basics—match content to the platform and provide insightful information that speaks to the personality of your firm—and go from there. Remember the following when planning your social media campaign:

Social Media is a great tool that reaches a huge audience. Paid advertisements on social media allow the marketer to select the specific audience intended to be reached. This form of marketing works well at the top of the funnel/beginning of the customer journey and helps channel traffic to your website. Social media changes frequently, and the platforms cater to various audience types. Be ready to pivot at all times. Do not stick with just one channel. Use the multi-channel approach to develop the right social media strategy for your law firm.

CHAPTER 10

MASS MEDIA

"Many a small thing has been made large by the right kind of advertising."

Mark Twain

While social media is an excellent way to reach and interact with a large audience on any kind of budget, the traditional forms of advertising still play a significant role in marketing strategies. TV, OTT (aka "Over the Top" advertising), radio, and print advertising continue to put your name and face in front of people—particularly those who may be less inclined to engage in social media. Traditional advertising is generally more costly and requires a team of creative professionals to produce the content for the ad slot. On top of those costs, you also have to weigh the costs of the ad slot itself.

For example, commercial time spots get a lot of notoriety around Super Bowl time, with the average cost ringing in at over $5.5 million. It's true that with all forms of traditional advertising, when, where, and how you put your law firm advertisement out into the world will dictate the price tag. That said, there is almost always room for a negotiation of rates.

If you have maxed out your customer journey, your referral strategy, and your digital strategy, it may be time to dive into mass media. Be sure it makes sense for your practice area. If mass media is not for your particular practice area, you may want to look into doubling down on marketing that is working or expanding into another geographical area. That analysis is not part of this book, but it is something I plan to explore in future writings.

The traditional forms of advertising still play a significant role in marketing strategies.

TV Advertising

Many wonder if TV advertising is on its way out of favor, but advertising on local TV stations will still reach an audience. If TV weren't a viable means of raising brand awareness, then politicians wouldn't ceaselessly annoy you during election years, and car dealerships wouldn't flash their hot deals between the weather report and the sports segment on your favorite local station. When Arby's pulls out of the TV ad game, then maybe it's time to reconsider, but as it stands, people do still watch TV—especially for the news and live sports. It's worth noting that older individuals hold most of the wealth in the country, and they also happen to watch the most television. They make an excellent target audience. TV is still a big part of the lives of many Americans. Do not discount this as a viable strategy for getting your name out into the community and creating a tremendous amount of awareness.

Another benefit of TV advertising has to do with the multi-tasking tendencies of Americans. While you might think our attention spans would detract from your TV ad, the benefit of someone always having a phone, laptop, or tablet in their hands when your ad airs is that they can enter a quick Google search of your firm when your firm's name is on their mind. They could easily land on your website, and more substantive content, all by virtue of your commercial.

There's a lot to consider after you've decided to run a TV ad. First and foremost, you need to know your budget. The main costs associated with a TV commercial are production and distribution. Production value matters, and it can cost anywhere from a few thousand dollars to tens of thousands of dollars. The cost of distribution is based on cost per thousand views and varies from market to market. For example, in Detroit, the cost-per-thousand views for a 60-second spot may be close to $18, but in Los Angeles, it is twice as much.

Do not skimp on the production of your commercial. Find the absolute best video production company to prepare a commercial that effectively communicates your brand and message but does so without losing the quality. A really high-end commercial is going to cost you at least $15,000 in some markets, and I have seen as high as $25,000. But the cost will return dividends as you blast the commercial hundreds of times per month to millions of people. If you are concerned about the production cost of a commercial, you are not ready to spend on TV.

TV advertising takes a great deal of money, time, and patience. This is not a direct response strategy. It is a long-term brand building strategy. My recommendation is you only jump into a channel if you plan on dominating the channel. This means you must find out what other competitors are spending on TV and be sure to outspend them or negotiate a better deal so that your ad gets the right amount of airtime. Frequency is the name of the game.

Over the years, I have seen many law firms jump into TV advertising and then give up three months in. Usually, it's because their advertising budget is only $5 to $10 thousand. Compare that to some firms in my area that spend upwards of $100,000 per month and you can see why it's hard to compete in the space. With that said, $10,000 spend on TV will work, if you are willing to put in 12 months of effort. The more money you can spend on mass media and getting eyeballs on your content, the faster and more successful your marketing will be. With that comes a tremendous amount of risk and patience to see it through.

The primary drawbacks of TV advertising are high costs and the limited ability to target an audience. It's also more difficult to access analytics that measure your ad's performance, which may prove frustrating when you're assessing your marketing budget and working to determine what's yielding a successful return on investment. That said, a successful TV commercial can provide thousands of viewers with 60 seconds of content that tells them why they need you. If you have the budget and the patience, I have seen this be an effective way to bring width to your organization.

A Note on Over-the-Top Advertising

OTT is short for over-the-top and refers to streaming commercials—aka those commercials that air during Hulu shows and YouTube videos and so forth. The production process and costs of OTT advertising are the same as in TV advertising, but there are some added benefits to streaming advertisements.

The benefit of OTT advertising is in the ability to target your audience more specifically. While TV advertising works to raise brand awareness near the top of the marketing funnel, OTT advertising is often targeted enough to engage individuals further down the funnel. While traditional TV advertising targets a broad and fairly unspecified audience, OTT can target viewers by city, county, zip code, and more. While production costs for OTT advertising are essentially the same as TV advertising, distribution costs are generally lower. Importantly, OTT advertising can be used to target younger audiences less inclined to catch the latest episode of Dateline on broadcast TV.

Radio Advertising

Like YouTube, I believe radio is an absolutely key part of driving massive awareness to your brand. I have personally witnessed immigration clients, family law clients, estate planning clients, and, obviously, personal injury clients respond to very good radio advertising.

Commercial advertising, either through traditional broadcast TV or digital streaming services, is a highly effective way to appeal to a large audience through visual narrative. However, the cost and time it takes to produce an effective video advertisement is no small task, and it may not even be an option for you right now. You could consider radio advertising as an alternative or a supplement to your marketing campaign, depending on your budget.

The key to radio is to know your target audience and pick the stations where your client is most likely going to be listening to the radio. You want to make sure that you are competitive on the station. Do not dip your toes into the water. The biggest mistake that law firm owners make is thinking that they can just test the channel. That is not how marketing works. Generally, you will need to be on the radio for at least nine to 12 months before you see any results. If frequency is the name of the game, you do not to start with a small spend because it will take even longer to have the kind of frequency that will lead to the awareness you need to be successful.

The more impressions you have on the radio, the more likely it will be that you can shorten the length of time you will have to play the radio spots before you are successful. Once you do reach the level of critical awareness, the leads will start coming in naturally because, again, people are predictable.

Radio spots are usually sold in 15, 30, or 60-second slots, and along with the length and the time of day of the airing, the station you wish to advertise on will together determine your distribution costs. To find the best audience for your firm, you need to research the radio stations in your region. If you provide malpractice defense, your more educated audience might prefer talk radio. If your firm litigates oil and gas interests in the southern states, the country stations are always a reliable niche. If you cater to estate planning legal needs, you'll find a receptive audience on the oldies stations.

In addition to radio commercials, you want to think of other assets the radio station may sell. Some of the more common assets could be sponsoring the traffic, weather, studio naming rights, and RDS. Some of these sponsorships are incredibly expensive, so you want to make sure you have a plan and strategy before you dive into spending on anything other than commercials.

The bottom line for mass radio advertising is that you need to pick the stations catering to your brand appeal audience, buy as much frequency as you can afford, think of all the assets the station may sell, and lastly, plan to be on the radio for one full year in a competitive spot before you make a determination that radio does or does not work.

I will save you the time and effort: it works if you follow the plan I listed above. In any channel you go into, be prepared to dominate the channel. That will lead to the greatest level of success.

Satellite and Subscription Radio Advertising

In addition to traditional radio advertising on your local broadcast stations, you could consider satellite radio advertising. This form of radio advertising reaches around 4 million subscribers, most of whom pay for the service, indicating perhaps a superior love for certain radio shows and a certain level of economic comfort. Most music-intensive channels on satellite radio are ad-free, which is a perk of the service. Still, some of the most beloved programming does sell ads, like Howard Stern and Doctor Radio. This specific area of radio advertising is extremely costly—about $15,000 per week.

A less expensive subscription base radio service is Pandora which had 80 million users as of 2020. While ad content is limited depending on the subscription type the user has, all users will experience ad content of some variety. The cost of advertising with Pandora is allocated based on how many people your ad is shown to by a metric of 1,000. WebFX.com explains, "The cost of advertising on Pandora varies, depending on the type of advertising you choose. Visual ads (which appear seven times per hour for most users) average $5 to $7 when calculated by CPM, or cost per million. This means that for every thousand people Pandora shows your ad, you'll be charged that amount."

Ultimately, the biggest tip of the trade in radio advertising is this: Repetition matters! Because you're only leaving an audio impression on an audience, you should run the ad several times. It should contain only one or two key impressions you want the listener to remember. Those listening to the radio are usually driving or performing some other task and are less likely than a visual audience to jot down the info.

Print Advertising

Print advertising is the use of billboards, newspapers, magazines, brochures, or direct mailers to spread awareness of your firm. As such, print advertising is widely adaptable to your ultimate campaign goals and budgets. Direct mail campaigns may include newsletters or big firm announcements. There are a variety of online spaces that will help you design and send bulk mailings at discounted rates. Check out Canva, for example.

You might wonder how relevant print advertising remains in the digital age. The truth of the matter is that you aren't wrong to ask—social media, television, and digital streaming reign supreme but your client focus may still be most receptive to print media. Niche industry magazines, for example, reach target audiences who've paid for the information provided therein. Additionally, reading enables a deeper connection with the media than an auditory or visual dissemination of information. Readers achieve higher engagement levels, particularly among those who've paid for the publication that contains the ad.

Some practice areas have seen phenomenal results with mailouts. I have been working with a bankruptcy lawyer who also helps people settle their debt due to a lawsuit and he is signing up 30 to 40 clients per month sending out letters in the mail to potential clients. Maybe it's the geographic area or the demographic he is targeting, but either way it works. The key to print is like any other channel you are using when developing your marketing campaigns and that is to identify your target audience and then ask where that audience can be found. Wherever they can be found is where you want to go.

Billboards

I'll make a short note here about billboard advertising—they work because they can't be avoided. A potential client can turn off the TV, shut down phone apps, put a magazine down, or change the radio station. They can't, however, unsee massive signage while driving down the highway. The cost of renting a billboard for display ranges from around $1,000 to $15,000 a month, depending on if you're in rural Kansas or New York City.

In 2019, despite great hesitancy, we launched an 80-billboard campaign in the city of Atlanta. The cost was insane. Prior to this, we had around five billboards, and they had not been that successful and so this was a true test. The six-month period of time before launching this new billboard campaign we had signed around seven new clients who directly attributed billboards as the reason they hired us. After we launched the campaign, that number rose to 158 which more than paid for the campaign itself. Billboards work, but, like everything else, you must have the intention of dominating the channel you are in.

Ultimately, the key to success in advertising is using your budget creatively and dynamically to reach a large and specific audience. As you've likely deduced, mass media advertising is quite a bit more expensive than its counterparts. It does, however, remain an effective way to reach a huge audience. Just remember the following:

Mass Media represents traditional forms of advertising in most cases. TV commercials, radio airtime, and print ads can reach a massive audience but are costly to produce and distribute. Still, the right ad will be highly effective. Although geared to a more traditional audience (i.e., older individuals), digital streaming and over-the-top advertising are effective with younger audiences who've cut the cable cord. While OTT can be specifically targeted, it's more difficult to target the other forms of mass media, which are focused on the time of day an ad airs or the type of publication in which you've placed the ad.

In the next few chapters, I'll walk you through methods that will help you launch your campaign and the key components that will enable you to make the most of your marketing methods.

CHAPTER 11

BUDGETING YOUR MARKETING CAMPAIGN

"We must consult our means rather than our wishes."

George Washington

I was working with a firm several years ago. Prior to them hiring me, the firm had routinely spent less than five percent on marketing and lead generation. Everything had come in through referrals and they were growing relatively fast. But something was happening, and the leads were slowing down. Growth was not taking place and they had become fearful. After having my discovery call, I knew the issue immediately was they had reached the max capacity of their referral network. They were building depth but did not have a very wide net. Depth was not producing more leads.

After carefully analyzing the marketing in their firm, we both instantly saw an opportunity to test some marketing. I made the recommendation for him to spend 25 percent in that one channel which he did not do. (The story of my consulting life). But he did increase his budget to 12.5 percent and I agreed it was not a bad start. Eight months later, without ever reaching the 25 percent mark, he hit his two best months in revenue and new clients and the momentum was clearly building. After he hit his best month ever for the second time, he called me and said, "You know, you may be right about this 25 percent thing." We both laughed and celebrated this amazing achievement.

Financial Controls

We have spent a lot of time on the fundamentals of growing your firm by starting to create momentum at the beginning of the law business funnel, which is marketing. I mentioned previously that there is a formula for growing your firm. Take another look at the economics of marketing chapter for review. When you operate using these techniques and you apply the proper spend, you will create momentum in lead generation that will drive the rest of the business.

We have now covered marketing opportunities within your budget while offering a plethora of tips for routing your message through the appropriate channels, paid or not. Now let's explore the money talk further. A key foundation of a successful marketing campaign is the completion of the campaign's vision. If you fall short of funds, you can't accomplish that. Even if you do have surplus resources, the foundation of creating and then managing an 8 Figure Firm is running all components as part of a well-oiled machine—including your marketing budget. Financial control, no matter the size of your spending, is crucial.

Part of financial controls is operating your business within ratios. Thirty-seven percent spent on people, 25 percent on marketing, 10 percent on operations, and the remaining amount on total owner's benefit. This formula should keep you growing at a fast pace while keeping your personal lights on. For many owners that have never jumped into the marketing space, this seems very difficult because they are accustomed to 50 percent profit margins. The legal industry has very large margins especially when the firms run on low overheads. The downside of living with a 50 percent profit margin is that you will never be able to scale a business like that. Sure, you may be able to grow to a significant size, but it will likely not have any predictability or system that can sustain it past your involvement.

One of my greatest achievements for my law firm has not been the size of the firm but rather the predictability of growth. That peace of mind comes from spending a consistent 25 percent into marketing and staying committed to running a law business not a law firm.

How to Allocate Your Budget

Nailing down your law firm's marketing budget can at first be an overwhelming process with a lot of moving parts. Depending on your touchpoint methodology, i.e., social media vs. mass media and so on, you'll want to account for the costs of production and distribution. There are some obvious costs associated with marketing—such as the expense of services provided by marketing professionals or the cost of buying airtime or ad space. An elevated approach to marketing budgets will also include the cost of time. For example, if you delegated certain tasks to support staff who might otherwise be billing on behalf of the firm for paralegal services, then that's an expense to be considered.

Some other costs of marketing include:

- Software

- Automation tools

- Trade shows and professional memberships

- Research

- Ghostwriters
- Content optimization and scheduling services
- Raw materials
- Thank you gifts

Nailing down a marketing budget often feels like pinning down a moving target. Each quarter you may reassess your generated income and realize that you need to pare down your marketing budget, refocus it, or add to it.

Below I will discuss an allocation plan that you can use to build your marketing budget.

The 60/40 Plan

I have already discussed the importance of spending at least 25 percent of your previous year's revenue on marketing. This will provide you the impressions and the leads necessary to sell enough to grow consistently and predictably. What do you do with the money you have now chosen to allocate towards marketing?

This is where I recommend the 60/40 plan. This plan recommends that you spend 40 percent of your budget on attracting sales today or what I call direct acquisition techniques. Pay per click, local services ads (Google Verified), referral fees, lead generation sites, all of these techniques are dedicated to getting your leads today. If you are reading this book, it is likely that you are not spending 25 percent of your revenue on marketing. When you jump into the marketing space, you want to make sure that any money you are spending is at a minimum being supplemented with immediate return.

This strategy alone is not sufficient. When you are buying leads in the direct attribution space, you will be competing with every other firm trying to buy those leads. It can get expensive quickly. What we know about clients that hire law firms from a pay per click ad is that they have zero brand loyalty to a law firm. If they had any brand loyalty, they would not have clicked on a paid ad. They would have called the brand they liked and trusted. This is a HUGE opportunity for you. As long as there are people hiring law firms with no brand loyalty, you have the opportunity to develop that brand loyalty for them.

The 60 percent is then going to be spent on brand building. Brand building is everything that helps create awareness of your brand but does not have a direct return on investment objective. The objective is just to get the marketplace to know, like and trust you. This strategy is for the long term. This is for the 97 percent of people who do not need a lawyer today but may need one in two years.

> **When you jump into the marketing space, you want to make sure that any money you are spending is at a minimum being supplemented with immediate return.**

I have run organic social media ads on Instagram for years. I make post and stories about the law firm sprinkled in between personal posts and stories. One day someone who had been following me for a couple years reached out and said, "Hey, do you do X type of injury cases?" I said of course.

From the moment that conversation happened until the day the case was resolved was 45 days. We settled the case for $300,000 and made $100,000 in revenue. All because of branding.

As you think about your spend, I would place 40 percent on direct response and 60 percent on branding to start off with. In a previous chapter you can find the allocation of several of my recommendations if you are looking for a place to start.

Utilizing the 70/20/10 Rule

Within the 60/40 rule is the 70/20/10 rule. A general rule of thumb for determining how to allocate your budget, whatever it may be or become, is the 70/20/10 rule. Essentially, following the 70/20/10 rule helps ensure that you're putting the bulk of your marketing resources toward proven techniques while still allocating a certain amount of your budget toward unproven marketing channels. According to the rule, 70 percent of your budget will go to channels that you know will yield a return on investment. Your ability to understand which channels are the most productive for you will depend on how closely you've tracked analytics relative to that marketing. If you aren't quite sure what tactics are yielding the most engagement, then now is the time to start figuring it out. Another way to find this out is to ask other lawyers who are in your practice area but are not in direct competition with you. This is where joining a mastermind group can be incredibly valuable. I have learned so much hearing from other lawyers in a mastermind setting. Some of the techniques have panned out and some have been total bombs. Knowing what has worked in the past has given me a guide to testing our market.

The way the 70 percent part of the rule would work is that 70 percent of your direct response budget (40 percent of your marketing budget) would go to proven techniques and 70 percent of your branding budget (60 percent of your marketing budget) would go to proven techniques. For example, if you had a $100,000 marketing budget, $40,000 would be spent on direct response and 60 percent would be spent on branding. Seventy percent of the $40,000 ($28,000) and 70 percent of the $60,000 ($42,000) would be spent on proven techniques.

While the bulk of your budget should go toward the methods you've found most effective, 20 percent of your budget should go to channels that may be less productive but still generate leads and engagement. These channels may be indirect but still provide quality exposure, like firm signage.

The way the 20 percent part of the rule would work is that 20 percent of your direct response budget (40 percent of your marketing budget) would go to proven techniques and 20 percent of your branding budget (60 percent of your marketing budget) would go to proven techniques. For example, if you had a $100,000 marketing budget, $40,000 would be spent on direct response and 60 percent would be spent on branding. Twenty percent of the $40,000 ($8,000) and 20 percent of the $60,000 ($12,000) would be spent on proven techniques.

The last 10 percent of your marketing budget is arguably the most fun to use as it creates room for experimentation and creative thinking. Dave Ramsey says, "A budget isn't about restricting what you spend; it gives you permission to spend without guilt or regret." It's important that you take some advertising risks, but it's often difficult to justify spending on unproven channels. When you've set aside a portion of your marketing budget specifically for exploration, you'll be more likely to enjoy it.

The way the 10 percent part of the rule would work is that 10 percent of your direct response budget (40 percent of your marketing budget) would go to proven techniques and 10 percent of your branding budget (60 percent of your marketing budget) would go to proven techniques. For example, if you had a $100,000 marketing budget, $40,000 would be spent on direct response and 60 percent would be spent on branding. Ten percent of the $40,000 (4,000) and 10 percent of the $60,000 ($6,000) would be spent on proven techniques.

Some areas of your budget are less obvious. For example, the return on investment may manifest outside of your budget spreadsheet. One way to ensure that you're placing value in the appropriate channels is to also consider your non-monetary successes and failures. Analytics accessed through Google, Facebook, and other spaces allow you to assign values to your goals, which facilitates a big picture perspective.

Staying Flexible and Managing Market Adjustments

A proactive budget plan will take you pretty far, but it's not the end-all-be-all of marketing success. To truly take the reins of your law firm's brand representation, you need to stay flexible. If the 2020s pandemic taught us anything, it's that the unforeseeable can happen. From disruption in daily life to changes in technology, there are any number of events that could ultimately thwart your marketing plans if you aren't at least mentally prepared to adapt. Flexibility ensures that resources will put your name and face in front of the right audience at the right time, but it also demonstrates your professionalism and agility to that audience. Jim Joseph of Entrepreuner.com said it succinctly when he wrote, "Remember that not all change is bad. In fact, when it comes to marketing planning, change is actually good. It's a good thing to be flexible and responsive and to have a finger on the pulse of what's going on with your business and be ready to respond to it. It's good to be ready so that you can be even more competitive."

All of this is true for marketing budgets. You need to have a financial plan but be prepared to make adjustments. Understanding your budget must-haves will help you reallocate costs from lower priority marketing plans if the need arises.

Ancillary Budget Considerations

Of course, sticking to a budget is important for the obvious reasons, but financial discipline serves a greater purpose than meeting the bottom line. It's important to think about marketing and your budget wholistically. Accurately tracking your resources ensures that you and your team are on the same page and that your funds contribute to a net positive feedback loop of marketing success.

Budgets Boost Team Morale

The preparation of a detailed marketing budget provides a set of clear expectations for your team. Team morale is almost always improved by focused priorities and goals achievable through actionable steps. A budget that provides your team with the tools they need to succeed will keep people motivated. It almost goes without saying that motivated teams perform better and stay more interested.

Tracking Marketing ROI

Marketing budgets also provide valuable aid in calculating your marketing ROI when used in conjunction with digital data analytics and traditional means of marketing analysis. Having a serious grasp of how your dollar is performing in every aspect of your marketing campaign means you can adjust strategies when and how you need to. There are a variety of ways to calculate your marketing ROI.

The **Money Out vs. Money In** calculation relies on the fairly simple strategy of computing the funds you spent on marketing in relation to the income the marketing campaign generates. While telling, this method can make it difficult to attribute the specific conversion rate per ad, since some clients may be sold on your firm right away while others need multiple touchpoints before they buy in. I would look at the return on investment from a wholistic perspective, not just from one channel. Looking at the return of investment for just TV could be deceiving. TV generally boosts web traffic, and many people do not directly attribute TV as their marketing source. Looking at the overall global cost of acquisition paints a much clearer picture. Additionally, what you are looking for is a minimum of a 5x return.

You may also want to consider a **Time Out vs. Money In** assessment because, as they say, time is money. If you, or those you've delegated the marketing tasks to, aren't adding value that would overcome the cost of the time taken away from other income-generating tasks, then you should take another look at your process. The goal *is* a net gain in the income generated, after all.

Marketing Cost Per Client is also a beneficial way of understanding your ROI. This approach considers the average cost of each client and provides perspective while answering questions about the value of your ads in relation to the value of your clients. Also known as "Client Acquisition Cost," this average should always take timing into consideration. For example, if you've opened a new office in a different part of your state, you can expect the marketing cost per client to be significantly larger for the same advertising you're disseminating in the region where you've already built some name recognition.

Diminishing Return Number

In addition to your client cost of acquisition, one of the most important numbers to track is your diminishing return number. This is the number that tells you what you can spend to acquire a case. We have now covered how much to spend on marketing. But how much should it cost to actually acquire a case? That number is 20 percent of your average attorney fee.

In practice, if your average attorney fee is $10,000, you should be willing to spend at least 20 percent on acquiring one case. If you have a practice where the average attorney fee is $5,000, your diminishing return should be $1,000 or less.

Why is this number important? When scaling your firm, you are going to be making more and more investments into marketing that will naturally raise your cost of acquisition. Knowing the number where you should stop making those investments is critical for you to pivot.

If you start aggressively marketing and your cost of acquisition rises from 10 percent of the average fee to 15 percent of your average fee, do you stop spending on marketing? NO!!! This is the time to keep going until you get to 20 percent. 20 percent that is where the return is less than five times, which is our target for legal services.

Each of the methods described above should be used dynamically to provide the big picture of how your marketing budget is working for you. Overall, the marketing budget is a crucial tool in your kit. When used with finesse, your allocation and tracking of resources is as much a part of the strategy as understanding who your client is and how best to attract them.

In summary, understanding the customer journey and how best to navigate it with specific marketing methods will be the crux of launching an effective marketing campaign. Further, without having your finger on the pulse of those matters, you will have a difficult time building and sticking to your firm's marketing budget. The budget is crucial for the obvious reason—you don't want to lose money. It's also a tool to provide you with insight into how effective your marketing investments are.

When you utilize your budget to unlock correlations between your marketing costs and your customer acquisition/retention, you'll be able to adjust your strategy to a larger effect. Allocate using the 60/40 Plan. Remember to stick to a 70/20/10 rule and allocate 70 percent of your budget toward proven marketing tactics; 20 percent to less direct strategies that still provide value; and 10 percent to new, unproven channels. Lastly, be sure your marketing return is five times your investment at all times.

CHAPTER 12

MAPPING YOUR MARKETING PLAN

"It's impossible to map out a route to your destination if you don't know where you're starting from."

Suze Orman

Early on in this book, I mentioned marketing funnels and provided a basic rundown of how they work. These funnels should serve as a blueprint for your overall marketing plan. To be sure, plans don't always go, well, to plan. That said, in the words of President Eisenhower, "Plans are useless, but planning is essential." Ultimately, marketing plans will enable you to set goals and assign value to various metrics that will help you understand your successes and analyze your failures. Your marketing map can be rudimentary to start, but as you dig in and design increasingly specific strategies to get where you want to go, the plan will take a more detailed shape. Importantly, plans enable adaptability. For example, you would look at a map before taking a long road trip (think pre-GPS). If your original route is unexpectedly closed for construction, you'd know what alternative routes are available because you have the map.

Even if you already have a marketing plan, there's considerable value in revisiting it now. Maybe you don't need to start from scratch but taking your vision back to the basics can help you see old channels in a creative new way, or new channels you hadn't originally considered.

To begin mapping your marketing plan, grab a paper and some pens and highlighters. Seriously. Draw out the funnel with the four main stages—Awareness, Interest, Consideration, and Conversion. Within each stage, brainstorm where you think your ideal client will encounter various touchpoints along their customer journey. At the top of the funnel, where the journey is most broad, you want to think about engaging a wide audience. Remember, you do want to direct your marketing to specific customer personas, but the top of the funnel should include all of those personas.

Touchpoints at the top of the funnel look like Google ads, TV commercials, billboard spots, digital TV ads, social media posts, guest lectures, and so on. As you move through the funnel, your middle touchpoints will focus on engagement with your leads. They may read through your website and blog articles, comment, or follow you on your social media pages. During this part of the customer journey, it's critical to remember that potential clients are weighing their options and comparing you to your competitors. When preparing your marketing map, be sure to consider arguments that demonstrate why your firm is the better choice. Outstanding reviews from current or past clients are helpful in understanding the client mentality.

Finally, at the bottom and most narrow point of the funnel, they'll reach out to you via your contact page, through chatbots, or maybe they'll give you a phone call if they like what they see and believe you can help them. Always follow up with the leads who reach out to you. This should go without saying, but if you haven't properly anticipated an influx of potential client interest after a big campaign push, you risk a breakdown in your ability to scale up. Mapping the plan should include your follow-up strategy. For example, how hard do you push your services if the lead is undecided? Should you include them in an email campaign if they tell you they aren't interested right now? The answer to that last question, by the way, is yes.

Refining Your Marketing Map

Once you've got an idea of what your firm's marketing funnel should look like, then you can work on building it out with specifics. Perhaps you already have a considerable amount of data to work with. If not, begin to collect the data now. The next step is to input your data into the mapping of your marketing plan. For each stage of the customer journey, include specific numbers and percentages. For example, what percentage of leads who visit your website end up at the conversion stage? If the percentage is low, where do the leads fall off? Do they drop off between the awareness level of the funnel and the interest level? If so, maybe you need to revamp your blog to speak more directly to your ideal customer personas. One way to do this is to rotate the articles you post so that you're engaging each customer persona consistently. If you're a criminal defense firm that handles a variety of case types, then don't only post articles about DUI's.

You'll be better able to answer the question of who is dropping off at which points if you've built out a marketing funnel with concrete numbers reflected at each stage. This provides a visual representation that enables you and your marketing team to set specific goals. In addition to your visual aids, you should also incorporate your CRM into this mapping process. Make sure you're logging inquiries and maintaining a sophisticated level of organization. CRM tools help you stay connected to your leads and provide data for you to build out your map.

Strategic Marketing Plan Sample

This is such an important part of the process that I did not want to leave you without a sample marketing plan. This plan was constructed for a law firm with over $5 million budget. The purpose for including this one was to give you the most possible information that you can see to then scale down for your budget.

Awareness Goals

- ❑ Improve awareness
- ❑ Increase web traffic & domain ranking
- ❑ Increase social engagement
- ❑ Get more news coverage
- ❑ Create more speaking opportunities
- ❑ Grow content marketing program
- ❑ Increase in-person engagement
- ❑ Improve voice ranking
- ❑ Create Talent Acquisition & Retention
- ❑ Increase "Community" Followers
- ❑ Grand Opening for all Offices

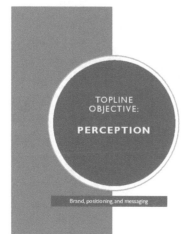

Perception Goals

- ❑ Improve Reputation (clients/future clients)
- ❑ Improve reputation (partners/future partners)
- ❑ Improve reputation (employees/future employees)
- ❑ Increase/improve online engagement
- ❑ Attain more company awards and accolades
- ❑ Become a thought leader: CLE Courses, Attorney Bar Speaking Engagements, Podcasts, Webinars
- ❑ Finalize rebrand/messaging/brand manual
- ❑ Complete brand alignment (graphics and copy writing)

Sales Goals 1

Goal	Metric of Achievement	Responsible Team/Ind.	Campaigns
Increase Referral Partners	52 new partners		Networking Dinners, Quarterly networking events, speaking engagements, happy hours, suite tickets/, partner database, gifting campaign
Increase Number of Referrals	2000 referrals		Clients- email campaigns, holiday & birthday cards, Former clients, Employees, Medical Providers, Law Firm, Friends & family
Increase Number of Leads	15000 leads		Anywhere, USA
Increase Conversion Rate of Leads	45% conversion of all leads		Certification program, Incentive program
Acquire/Increase number of cases	5200 cases		Anywhere, USA

Mapping Your Marketing Plan

Sales Goals 2

Goal	Metric of Achievement	Responsible Team/Ind.	Campaigns
Reduce Acquisition Costs	Reduce to $1,200		
Reduce Churn Rate	3%		Client Journey
Build & Grow contact databases	10,000 – clients 10,000 – industry professionals		List purchase/Downloads Lawyers, MDs, nurses, PTs, Chiros, Updates/Download client lists See Referral campaigns
Grow New Sales Channels	250 Social Media cases		Paid social
Increase Satellite office cases	250 cases		New offices, USA

QUALITATIVE GOALS: SALES

Awareness Goals

Goal	Metric of Achievement	Responsible Team/Ind.	Campaign
Talent Acquisition & Retention	52 posts per IG, FB, LI $6000/yr on Paid Social 4 Networking Events		Organic Social Media Paid Social Media Networking Events
Create Speaking Engagements	12 engagements Min 1 per lawyer		Bar Association/CLEs
Increase web traffic & Domain ranking	TBD		SEO
Increase Social Engagement	TBD		Engagement $ Followers (FB,IG,LI)
Increase News Coverage	TBD		Press Releases
Improve voice search optimization	TBD		SEO, Siri, Yelp
Increase in-person engagement	10,0000 contacts in database/ invite lists		Community events Networking Sponsorship Activations
Increase "community" followers	5,000 followers		Social Media/Traditional Media

QUALITATIVE GOALS: AWARENESS

Perception Goals I

Goal	Metric of Achievement	Responsible Team/Ind.	Campaign
Perceived as Top Place to Work	12 Awards 52 reviews per platform Testimonials Quarterly Employee Surveys		Website Landing Page HR Marketing Audit (website, Social Media, LinkedIn Business page) Award & Accolades Reviews & Testimonials Employee Surveys
Improve Reputation (clients)	1500 reviews (1200 Google) 52 Testimonials MH/Super Lawyers 100% application		Testimonials, Google, Facebook, Yelp, BBB Reviews, MH/Super Lawyers Surveys, Gifting, Copy Messaging
Improve Reputation (employees)	100 Glassdoor Reviews 100 Indeed Reviews 100 EE Videos		Testimonials, Google, Facebook, Yelp, BBB Reviews, MH/Super Lawyers Surveys, Gifting, Copy Messaging
Improve Reputation (partners)	5% of revenue per partner		Gifting

QUALITATIVE GOALS: PERCEPTION

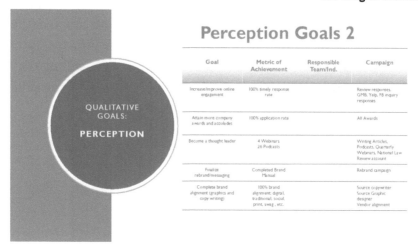

Perception Goals 2

Goal	Metric of Achievement	Responsible Team/Ind.	Campaign
Increase/improve online engagement	100% timely response rate		Review responses, GMB, Yelp, FB inquiry responses
Attain more company awards and accolades	100% application rate		All Awards
Become a thought leader	4 Webinars, 26 Podcasts		Writing Articles, Podcasts, Quarterly Webinars, National Law Review account
Finalize rebrand/messaging	Completed Brand Manual		Rebrand campaign
Complete brand alignment (graphics and copy writing)	100% brand alignment: digital, traditional, social, print, swag, etc.		Source copywriter, Source Graphic designer, Vendor alignment

QUALITATIVE GOALS:

PERCEPTION

Patience in the Process

After you've mapped out your marketing plan in detail, your work is still not over. In fact, your work is never really over, because the key to success in building an 8 Figure Firm is continuous optimization. Again, that doesn't mean you need to burn the midnight oil for the duration of your professional career. What it means is that you and your marketing team need to keep a finger on the pulse of what's driving your firm's marketing successes. There is a lot of room for task delegation here, and the bigger your firm grows, the more resources you'll have to invest in people and software that can help you.

The mapping process does require a certain amount of patience. The most successful marketing strategies necessitate a long-term vision and a willingness to collect data over time in order to adjust your plan as needed. A successful marketing campaign is more than buying Google Ads. It's an intuitive understanding of where the holes are in your marketing plan and then rerouting the path on your map to avoid those holes. Importantly, there's always the chance that a shift in a strategy designed to improve conversion rates will still end with disappointing results. While frustrating, this data matters too.

With each failure, the path to success becomes clearer by virtue of the process of elimination. Finance guru Dave Ramsey aptly said, "Success is just a pile of failure that you are standing on," and all truly successful people would probably agree—I know I do.

CHAPTER 13

EXECUTING YOUR MARKETING PLAN

"Execution is a specific set of behaviors and techniques that companies need to master in order to have competitive advantage. It's a discipline of its own."

Ram Charan and Larry Bossidy

When working with clients, I constantly repeat, "Speed of growth is tied to speed of implementation." They go hand in hand. You can't grow quickly without doing things fast and pivoting fast. Preparing your team for growth is all about preparing them for speed of implementation. To begin your scale process, you must create a tremendous amount of implementation speed at the marketing stage of your business. Without successful execution on the strategies discussed and a well-defined marketing plan, you will stay in the wishful thinking stage. As I am sure you may have heard before, hope is not a strategy.

Discussing the execution of your marketing plan goes hand in hand with the process of mapping your marketing plan. In many ways, you cannot do one without the other—they are both parts of the big picture required of 8 Figure Firm marketing success. That said, planning is all about the potential of your success, while execution is about the doing. You can plan until the cows come home, but that doesn't mean you'll have milk on the table. In order to avoid wasting the time and resources you've put into making your plan and missing opportunities to grow, you need to take actionable steps to execute your vision.

Step 1: Put the Marketing Team Together

Back in the first few chapters of this book, I mentioned that one of the key components of the marketing mindset is knowing what your strengths and weaknesses are. Depending on where you are in your understanding of your marketing abilities, you may already suspect you'll need assistance in certain areas. Perhaps you'll need help updating your firm's Facebook page with engaging content, or maybe you don't have time to commit to the CRM software tools. Identifying where you need help allows you to reinforce your weak areas.

Let me clarify that by "marketing team," I mean any number of setups. You can outsource to professional marketing services if you have the resources, or you could keep the marketing in-house if you have a star support staffer or two who can take on the additional workload. You could also hire someone to work internally. All of the above situations constitute the marketing team. The key to efficiently and effectively building the team that suits your firm best is in understanding which of your marketing strategies are non-negotable to start with. Then go from there. For example, your firm needs to have a website, but websites take various forms. If you're using Wix or Squarespace or a plug-and-play platform to host your site, you need a content manager or website designer to build and maintain your content so that it's explanatory, accurate, and easy to navigate. If you have a custom site, then you'll need a website designer and developer (and probably a content manager, too) to design, build, and maintain the site.

Who you need on your marketing team will be specific to your firm's needs at any given moment. Hiring the right team member or members for the job is critical in executing your marketing plan.

When you first start out, it is tempting to try to do everything yourself. When I launched my firm, I did the same thing. I did not have any money and had to put in a lot of sweat equity. I was working 18-hour days almost every day of the week, working on developing business, networking and creating content for my site. As I started getting a little bit more money, I began outsourcing many of those tasks because I did not have enough work to bring everything in house. The biggest mistake law firm owners make with marketing personnel is believing they can manage an in-house team in the early stages of the business. If you are not a gifted CMO, it is likely that your time and money will be better spent hiring specialists to take on the work for you. Here is what a sample team would look like:

Marketing Stakeholders

Step 2: Set Achievable Goals

At the beginning of each year our firm starts with the company goals. The goals are statements of things we want to achieve, such as building a client-centric organization or establishing a dominant presence in the general market. These goals begin to inform us of what we have to do in order to succeed in the year. Once the goals have been established, we carve out marketing needs to take place in order to achieve those goals. The next step will be where we break down each part of the goal into achievable quarterly goals for the marketing so that we have benchmarks for the business to hit.

Discussing the execution of your marketing plan goes hand in hand with the process of mapping your marketing plan.

Setting achievable goals serves two purposes: firstly, goals give your team direction, and secondly, goals move your team forward while letting them measure their progress. There are numerous ways you can set goals for yourself and your team. Google Analytics provides goal templates and also allows for custom goals. Of course, you can also develop your goals the old-fashioned way or consult with marketing professionals who can help you develop goals that will boost momentum. Examples of marketing goals include:

- Gain a target percentage of social media shares
- Publish a specified number of blog articles per month
- Increase website traffic by a target percentage
- Record a certain number of videos for content

- Develop a specific number of new vendor relationships

- Develop a specific number of new lead sources by a certain date

These examples are listed in no particular order, and they certainly aren't exhaustive, but they do provide an idea of the types of goals that offer concrete metrics. Some of your goals, like "build more success" or "make more money," for instance, make for great mantras, but they're relatively esoteric, and you may never actually know if you've reached them. Those broad goals point you in the direction you want to head, but they don't offer you the tangible mile markers you need to evaluate your progress. Teams that can't evaluate their progress lose focus, interest, and motivation—all of which are execution kryptonite.

Step 3: Allocate Time

Another roadblock many law firm managers run into is setting aside the amount of time required for the effective execution of their marketing strategies. Most extremely successful individuals get a lot done in a day, not because they've unlocked the secret to stopping the clock, but because they understand time management. One of the tricks of the trade is to start by estimating the amount of time it's going to take to accomplish certain tasks and setting aside time out of the day to do the tasks. You're undoubtedly familiar with the billable hour and so timeboxing strategies should be somewhat intuitive.

A Lucidchart.com article sums up timeboxing by saying, "Contrary to most productivity practices where an individual takes on a task and works at it until completion, timeboxing is a time management technique that limits a task to a fixed (but realistic) timeline that may be minutes, hours, days, or even weeks long, depending on the task complexity." Notably, Bill Gates is a proponent of this time management strategy.

The most important thing to understand if you want to dominate your marketing is that you, the law firm owner, must put as much time as possible into your marketing and sales. Being a good lawyer will never allow you to dominate the market. Getting good results will not lead to dominating your market. The only thing that will lead to dominating your market is implementing the strategies I have laid out in this book and focusing on creating an incredible amount of momentum at the beginning of your law business funnel. When you are also a practicing lawyer, this can be incredibly challenging. The sooner you can delegate the legal work and focus on the marketing, the sooner you will be building and scaling your law firm.

Regardless of which team member will be executing the tasks, understanding the time allocation for each activity will help you carve out time. Start with an estimate and consider taking notes—was your original time allotment too short? Too long? Was it probably the right length of time, but you found you were interrupted on three separate occasions? If the latter is the case, maybe it's time to delegate that particular task. Timeboxing is an effective way to manage the execution of your marketing objectives incrementally.

Step 4: Make Checklists and Set Deadlines

This one may be obvious, but it's worth a brief discussion. Few things in life are as satisfying to the goal-oriented individual as checking something off a to-do list or meeting a deadline. Put your marketing goals and objectives into calendars and use tech tools available to share the task lists and deadlines with your marketing team. Even when you've outsourced to professionals, these tools will ensure that everyone is on the same page and working to execute the marketing plan within the agreed-upon timeline and vision parameters. If you're just getting your feet wet in managing teams and marketing plans, then you can download affordable team management software like Asana, Trello, or Airtable and utilize the free trials to determine which may work best for your firm's needs.

Putting deadlines into calendars not only ensures that your team finds clarity in your marketing expectations, but also allows you to consider your long-term plans. In the words of Jeff Bezos, "If we think long term, we can accomplish things that we wouldn't otherwise accomplish. Time horizons matter. They matter a lot."

If you want to use an old school Google sheet to keep track, you can do something like this:

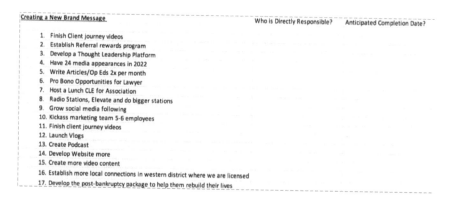

Step 5: Preparing to Scale Up

For as long as you're planning to grow your firm, you can expect to continue executing your marketing plan. It can be a trial-and-error process, but once your marketing machine is up and running and off the races, you shouldn't be surprised when you start seeing truly explosive growth. At this point, there are only a few things that can bring it all crashing down, but a failure to scale up is probably the most common. What happens if you take on an influx of clients but you're ill-equipped to manage their needs? Best case scenario—you have some upset clients who take their business elsewhere and tell their friends to avoid your firm. Worst case scenario—you end up looking for an attorney of your own to represent you in a malpractice lawsuit.

Preparing to scale up after a successful marketing initiative can feel a lot like bracing for the storm. While your goal is obviously to grow, it will be hard to predict exactly when and how the influx will hit. To soften the blow, plan to do the following:

- Develop a hiring plan based on anticipated growth.

- Hire support staff and associates before you need them; if you aren't ready to hire, then consider contracting attorneys and staff or even VA's to take on some administrative work.

- Streamline training processes for new hires.

- Invest in scalable tech tools (like data storage) and have heavy workflow processes in place.

- Be prepared to outsource processes like payroll, client billing, settlement disbursements, etc.

- Have a plan for expanding your physical office space or strategize remote work options.

Ultimately, each firm's growth will take shape in different ways, and in keeping with the sentiment I've often repeated in earlier chapters, the name of the game is to be prepared and stay flexible.

CHAPTER 14:

MEASURING THE SUCCESS

"If you can't measure it, you can't improve it."

Peter Drucker

I've written about the importance of marketing analytics throughout this book, but I want to take some time to focus exclusively on measuring the success of your marketing campaign. Some of the terms I've included in this chapter will sound familiar, but it's imperative that you have a working knowledge of them. Most law firms measure the success of their marketing campaign only by increases in their revenue. If revenue goes up, then your marketing worked, right? Similarly, if your revenue went down, then the basic assumption is that the marketing campaign was a failure.

Other law firm owners try to measure everything through direct attribution. If I spend $10,000 in this marketing channel, then I should get this amount of clients from that channel. That is similarly a bad way to look at your marketing.

The truth is that revenue isn't always the best measurement of how effective your marketing campaigns were in a given year nor is direct attribution. Outside factors can contribute to law firm growth or stagnation despite successful marketing campaigns. Bad years happen for various reasons, including pandemics, inflation, global crisis, and so on. You shouldn't measure success based solely on one number at the end of the fiscal year. The thinking is similar to investing in the stock market. The savvy investor doesn't worry about one bad year because they know that they'll see growth over a ten-year average. Similarly, those working to grow their law firm into an 8 Figure Firm should measure the success of their marketing initiatives over the long term.

The greatest measurement of your marketing is not revenue growth, although everyone wants the revenue to grow, nor is it direct cost of acquisition, although we want to know this also. The greatest measurement is how predictable your lead generation is. The more predictable your development of new client becomes, the more successful your marketing will be.

Imagine a business that could with great certainty predict how many new clients they would generate in any given year based upon spend. Don't think it's possible? You would be completely wrong. After many years of spending 25 percent of our revenues on marketing, our firm has accomplished just that. We have managed to predict how many new clients we can generate over a period of time. That level of predictability has led to predictable need for new hires, predictable revenues, and ultimately predictable profit. We are so confident in these metrics that we normally set our total owners benefit at the beginning of the year and pay ourselves that way.

Last year we predicted our revenue with almost 97 percent accuracy. To me that is the best metric of all.

over Budget	% of Budget
-140,807.41	32.95%
3,158.13	
426,199.02	119.37%
-181,558.94	37.39%
53,002.67	132.32%
3,704.40	106.23%
-359,502.46	92.14%
-$ 195,804.59	97.39%

Using Key Performance Metrics (KPI) to Measure Marketing Campaign Success

KPI is the broad umbrella term used to describe all metrics used in determining how well your marketing campaign is performing. Measuring campaign success, or lack of success, provides critical insight. The more detailed the measurements you track are, the better you'll be able to enhance your return on investment (ROI) by cutting out unnecessary spending and reallocating your budget to methods that are working better. Below I'll discuss some important terms commonly used in evaluating KPI. Notably, many of these apply to online marketing as online platforms dominate today's marketing world.

Conversion Rate

Understanding your conversion rate is important for determining how successful your marketing campaign has been in guiding potential clients through their customer journey. The conversion rate speaks to your success in moving a lead to act in a specific way. Some actions that constitute a conversion can include clicking a link that takes the lead to your website, making a phone call, or signing a client agreement. As such, you can use the conversion rate to evaluate numerous points along the customer journey. For example, if ten leads visit your website and five of them call your firm, the conversion rate for that step is 50 percent.

The more predictable your development of new client becomes, the more successful your marketing will be.

Depending on your practice area, your conversion rate can vary greatly. In personal injury and other types of contingency practices, you should expect a conversion rate of 90 percent or more of all viable leads. In cash-based law practices where you ask for a flat fee or a retainer, I believe you should convert between 50 percent and 70 percent of viable leads. Some of you may be wondering, "But what if they don't have the money?" That question usually comes from law firm owners who don't know how to sell.

Value Perception Concept

I want to answer the question from the last section by explaining the concept of value perception. When clients tell you they do not have the money, what they are really saying is that you did not sell them on the value of the service you are providing. We know this to be true because, as explained earlier in this book, those same people never seem to have any problem buying $2,000 to 3,000 handbags.

I remember one time I saw someone on Facebook asking for help. They had fallen on hard times and could not pay their electric bill. They said if anyone could help them pay the bill, they would greatly appreciate it. I felt compelled and called the local power company. I told them that all I wanted to do was pay the bill for this person. The bill may have been $100. Several days later, I saw this same person post on Facebook that they were heading to Disneyland. I was furious. I realized in that moment that people will find ways to pay for the things they want and value.

I will give you another example. If you had no money and a dealership told you they would sell you a Lamborghini for $15,000, would you find the money to buy it? Of course you would. The perception of value for the car is so high that you would have no choice but to find a way.

When I sell consulting services and I fail to convert the client because of the money objection, the first thing I ask myself is where I failed to deliver on value. I use that moment to revise my pitch and improve on it the next time. As it stands, I convert almost 80 percent of all attorneys that call 8 Figure for services. It's all about value perception.

Costs Per Lead (CPL)

CPL speaks to how many leads are generated by a certain dollar amount. This metric doesn't focus on how much revenue is generated from a campaign, but rather on how much of your budget resulted in a new lead. This is the first part of your cost per acquisition analysis. If your cost of acquisition is rising, you should analyze your cost per lead first to see if maybe you are not generating enough leads to get the conversions you need.

Costs Per Click (CPC)

CPC is the dollar amount spent on paid advertising divided by the number of clicks resulting from that advertising. Often, the third party offering the paid advertising will charge the law firm by click. Paying a third party on a CPC basis is common with Facebook and Instagram advertising. Essentially, the online platform will boost your posts to a broader audience, and if someone clicks on that post, you pay for the click.

Costs Per Acquisition (CPA)

The CPA metric calculates the costs spent to acquire a new client. While CPA appears a simple equation at first, it proves a moving target in practice, as there are direct and indirect costs associated with new client acquisition.

When fine-tuning your marketing budget, you'll want to know the cost of case acquisition. Sometimes this measurement can be tricky, especially for firms that tend to market more heavily. To understand where you need to go, you first need to understand your base year cost of case acquisition. If you aren't sure what your base year cost of case acquisition is, you could research industry standards, make an informed estimate, or use the 20 percent rule. The 20 percent rule assumes the cost of case acquisition is 20 percent of your average fee.

The goal for your cost of acquisition is to be 20 percent or less of your average attorney fee. As you dominate your market, you will want to make sure to keep stacking marketing initiatives to increase awareness and impressions. This will ultimately lead to a higher global cost of acquisition. It will also increase your visibility and leads.

Customer Lifetime Value (LTV)

LTV tells us the average revenue generated from one client for the duration of their engagement with your firm. Some clients only need to hire a firm for a single matter, while others will keep coming back. From a marketing perspective, client retention is great because return clients don't require much CPA allocation.

Outsourcing Your Marketing Campaign Analysis

You might wonder if you should do your own campaign analysis or if you should hire a third party to help you analyze your KPI. This decision is a matter of resources. Ask yourself if you have the time *and* the budget to hire a third party. If your honest answer is yes to both factors, then you should feel free to outsource the task to experts. There is no shortage of marketing companies who would love your business, so ensure you do your research before hiring. Even when you hire someone else to manage your marketing campaigns, though, it's wise to have a working knowledge of the metrics.

If you'd like to start out doing your own KPI, there are plenty of online resources you can use to fine-tune your understanding of marketing analytics. You could also take a seminar. The important thing to remember when you choose to DIY the analysis is that you need to regularly check in and make adjustments when your efforts experience ups or downs.

You might find you thoroughly enjoy driving your marketing machine and choose to remain behind the wheel for the long haul. On the other hand, you might ultimately decide to hand the reigns over to someone else and allow yourself the freedom to check in only as needed. Find a process that works for you and your firm.

CHAPTER 15

THE CONVERSION

*"Every sale has five basic obstacles: no need,
no money, no hurry, no desire, no trust."*

Zig Ziglar

At the very bottom of the marketing funnel lies the coveted conversion stage. This is the moment you've worked so hard for and the time when you finally see a return on investment in your financial and temporal resources. In the legal sphere, the client base is uniquely poised to need your services. Hiring a lawyer is almost never a completely spontaneous decision, which is both good and bad. On the one hand, those who are looking for legal help will be actively researching you and your competitors. As a result, your leads will be more apt to skip down to the narrower stages of the marketing funnel. On the other hand, your potential client base will be specifically focused and may be easily dissuaded if they don't think your services align with their needs. As you now know, developing client personas will help you target these situationally limited leads from the get-go. But what happens when they reach the bottom of the marketing funnel?

The Conversion

Law firms will most successfully turn a potential client into an actual client when the firm can:

- Demonstrate expertise in the required legal niche.
- Represent a team of dedicated support staff and attorneys.
- Communicate compassionately and effectively.
- Match their value to the costs of the services provided.

It's important to understand that some clients will have a high need, and some will have a low need. As you can probably guess, the low-need clients will move through conversion, with most of their concern centering on the cost of legal services. The high-need clients will be more ready and willing to pay if they feel they're being offered better overall value from you than your competitors. If your marketing campaign has been successful, and all of your touchpoints have demonstrated the first three bulleted points, then the last bulleted point is where you'll see most potential clients balk.

In conversation with the hesitant client, you should leverage the first three points to justify the cost of your services to the lead. Generally, your cost per billable hour will be similar to that of similarly sized firms in your region. The lead who calls around to research fees isn't likely to find a discount significant enough to overcome your demonstration of competence and attention to their needs, so long as you've adequately demonstrated such. When you understand your value and can convey that value to the potential client, you're apt to see them funnel all the way through to conversion. Then, with a job well done, they will filter through the entire marketing funnel over and over again, and they will send their friends and family your way as well.

Some potential clients simply aren't that motivated. They may see a need for your services, but it's not time-sensitive.

Estate planning attorneys see a lot of this. There are a few approaches you can take when you encounter a low-need client—if you leave a lasting impression, they will remember the free consultation you gave them once they become more motivated to receive legal help. Alternatively, you could offer them a discount and secure them as clients now. What you decide to do ultimately depends on how badly you want and need new clients. Highly motivated clients who have a legal need that must be addressed right away will often be the clients that end up offering the most gratitude. Remember, gratitude translates to referrals and repeat business.

> **When you understand your value and can convey that value to the potential client, you're apt to see them funnel all the way through to conversion**

Create Urgency

A sales tactic I have seen work really well is to create urgency. Creating urgency can mean something different for different practice areas. In the personal injury space, it could mean that if a client waits too long they will have a gap in treatment and the insurance company will deny their claim. In the estate planning area I will tell the story of a family member who did not leave a will; the family did not know what to do after they passed and had to go through the trouble of figuring it out. In immigration it could be that the laws are always changing and you need to act fast so that you don't later get excluded by a change in the law.

There is always a reason for the person to act with a sense of urgency. You need to help them see why it is urgent to act.

The Conversion

While conversion is the last component of your marketing campaign, it does not signal the end of the customer journey. If you've done your marketing job right, the customer will move through the funnel again and again and again. Of course, some law practices are better suited for repeat customers. Still, while estate planning or real estate attorneys are more apt to see clients walk back through the door than criminal defense attorneys, all firms should provide the type of customer service and client support that would entice a client to move through the funnel all over again.

Prepare For Objections

The reason that you or your sales team have a difficult time with conversion is that you are not prepared for the objections. We all know what objections we commonly hear for our services. We know if it's a money thing, or a time thing, or something else.

Preparing for these objections can help you eliminate some of these misses. What I recommend is that you start by listing the objections that you hear most often. Once you have them named, write out a clear answer to the objection.

Once objection might be, "I need to talk to my spouse." You must have a prepared answer for that objection.

The final step in preparing for the objections is to rehearse the answer over and over so it naturally becomes part of the conversation. Sometimes even bringing up the objection at the beginning will eliminate it. Start the conversation with, "I know you may be thinking you need to speak to your spouse about this but..."

Not only will this help overcome the objections more often than not, but having the common objections written down with the rehearsed answers will allow you to train your sales team much more effectively.

Additional Means of Conversion

I want to point out that conversion can happen at several points along the customer journey. Of course, the most significant conversion point is when the potential client hires you to do legal work, but you shouldn't ignore the other conversions. A conversion simply means that a lead has made a decision to move to the next step in the customer journey. Additional examples of conversion include:

- Deciding to click on a social media post to read more

- Responding to and interacting with a social media post

- Following a link in an email that leads to a blog post

- Subscribing to your blog

- Calling your law firm after seeing your commercial on TV

- Filling out the contact form on your website

Every action a lead makes as a result of your marketing campaign is a conversion, and it's just as important to take stock of these smaller milestones as it is to celebrate the final conversion. All of these small conversions should be used as touchpoints for retargeting and remarketing to those potential clients. Over time, they will become clients or will make referrals so do not discount them.

The final conversion, when the lead becomes a client, is the culmination of each conversion along the way. Marketing without sales will not work. Pay extremely close attention to your conversion rates.

Tying it Together

To tie the last few chapters about marketing campaigns together: Budgets will help you understand how you want to map your marketing plan and how you need to allocate resources to the marketing stages. With data collected through CRM software and digital analytic tools, you can develop a high-level plan that provides tangible goals and a big picture view of where you need improvement. It's difficult to execute the marketing plan without first mapping your anticipated journey.

While it may be possible, it's extremely unlikely that you'll find the kind of 8 Figure Firm success you're looking for without a roadmap. Remember that in the execution of your marketing plan, you need to develop tangible goals in addition to your big-picture objectives and themes. These specific goals provide direction, prove momentum, and add an element of a job well done to boost the entire team's morale. If your marketing strategy has gone according to plan, then you end up at the bottom of the marketing funnel with customer conversion in sight. Here you need to leverage your firm's value to the potential customer. Depending on the severity of the person's need, they'll weigh the cost with the services you can provide. It's your time to shine and close the deal. As your marketing picks up, and in turn, so does your client base, ensure scalability so that all of those new clients become repeat clients and referral sources.

CONCLUSION

"The reward for work well done is the opportunity to do more"

Jonas Salk

I spent most of my life trying to figure out what I was good at. I wanted more than anything to be a professional baseball player. Despite my father playing Double-A ball in Puerto Rico and me inheriting some level of talent, I could never overcome the injuries I suffered throughout my college career. Despite these injuries and the subsequent surgeries I needed to correct the damaged those injuries caused, I stayed resilient and finished my four years of college baseball.

This resiliency has been the greatest asset I could have ever asked for. It has allowed me to endure hard times and hard moments. Moments I felt I might never recover from. Resiliency has taught me that if you are willing to stay the course long enough, you will win at this game of life and business.

As a person of faith, many years ago I was confronted with several life changes that led me to see a Christian counselor.

During that time, I was asked a question that completely changed my life.

"Who do you become when you become who God created you to be?"

I will never forget that question. For years I was wrestling with who I was as an individual. Who was I meant to be? What would my story be? After six weeks of thinking about these questions, I settled on an answer.

When I became who God created me to be, I became powerful, walking in His purpose for my life. For me that changed everything. When I realized the power I had in this understanding, I decided that a life full of power required a plan and intention.

This entire book comes from the desire to build intentional lives where we have some level of predictability. I hope that in this book, you too will find your power in creating the life you want and becoming the king of growth in your market.

For those who are motivated and driven to take the reins of their firm's marketing machine, an 8 Figure Firm can be a reality. By reading this book, you've already taken steps to build your marketing machine. Congratulations! Here's what we've learned:

- We discussed the need for understanding the *economics of law firm growth* in gauging the success of your marketing campaigns.

- We discussed the importance of a *marketing mindset* to help you embrace the journey in a creative and exciting way.

- We discussed how and why you should *define your law firm brand* to boost audience engagement.

- We discussed how to clarify the *customer journey* so your marketing campaigns run effectively and efficiently.

- We discussed the importance of *marketing campaigns and channels* in effectively conveying your brand message.

- We discussed *managing marketing funnels* and the importance of organizing and utilizing data.

- We discussed *referral marketing* and how momentously effective word-of-mouth marketing is.

- We discussed *social media marketing* and how each platform should direct a different tone of voice to a different audience, and how effective engagement can reach a massive audience with the click of a button.

- We discussed *mass media* and how it's best wielded as a tool to reach certain audiences in specific locations.

- We discussed the reasons you need to *budget for your marketing campaign* and how there are non-monetary benefits to the budgeting process.

- We discussed how to *map your marketing plan* and why data analytics will help you overcome inefficiencies.

- We discussed why *executing your marketing plan* is best achieved through teamwork and time management strategies.

- We discussed how and why you need to *measure the success of your marketing campaign* so you can build and maintain law firm growth.

- We discussed *conversion* and how the final stage of the customer journey will look different depending on a customer's motivations.

Conclusion

These marketing strategies work, and we know because we used them to build our **PREDICTABLE** $30 million and growing firm. As noted in the introduction of this book, it took a lot of trial and error to get to where we are, and if there's one thing we can pass along, it's the ultimate success story and how we did it. If you follow our lead and begin to work these processes into your own marketing journey, there's no reason you, too, can't grow to an 8 Figure Firm.

Although you can take this information and hit the ground running with it without any additional help from us, having experienced advisors walk this path of success with you can also be valuable. If you're interested in delving deeper into our resources, we offer a variety of services to help you develop these principles even further. We provide one-on-one coaching and expert programs to open your door to success even wider. To learn more about how we can help you build momentum on your path to growing your firm, visit us at www.8figurefirm.com or contact us through our contact page.

TO YOUR CONTINUED SUCCESS!

ABOUT THE AUTHOR

Luis Scott is a nationally renowned lawyer, speaker, and consultant in the field of law firm growth. His concepts of intentionality in law firm building and having a plan and design for sustainable and predictable growth has led to hundreds of lawyers experiencing the power of true scale for their law firms. With a background din Accounting and Law, Luis takes his school experience and his 20 years journey in the legal profession and show you how he built his own law firm to multiple 8 Figures in predictable revenue.

Visit: www.8figurefirm.com for free tools and resources on building your law firm.